Dido Queene of Carthage

and

Massacre at Paris

Christopher Marlowe

Contents

The Tragedy of
Dido Queen of Carthage

Written by

CHRISTOPHER MARLOWE
and
THOMAS NASH

1594

The text is from the Bodley copy.

Actors

Iupiter.
Ganimed.
Venus.
Cupid.
Iuno.
Mercurie.
Hermes.
Æneas.

Ascanius.
Dido.
Anna.
Achates.
Ilioneus.
Iarbas.
Cloanthes.
Sergestus.

The Tragedie of Dido
Queene of Carthage

Here the Curtaines draw, there is discovered Iupiter *dandling*
Ganimed *upon his knee, and* Mercury *lying asleepe.*

Iup. Come gentle *Ganimed* and play with me,
I loue thee well, say *Iuno* what she will.

Gan. I am much better for your worthles loue,
That will not shield me from her shrewith blowes:
To day when as I fild into your cups,
And held the cloath of pleasance whiles you dranke,
She reacht me such a rap for that I spilde,
As made the bloud run downe about mine eares.

Iup. What? dares she strike the darling of my thoughts?
By *Saturnes* soule, and this earth threatning aire,
That shaken thrise, makes Natures buildings quake,
I vow, if she but once frowne on thee more,
To hang her meteor like twixt heauen and earth,
And bind her hand and foote with golden cordes,
As once I did for harming *Hercules.*

Gan. Might I but see that pretie sport a foote,
O how would I with *Helens* brother laugh,
And bring the Gods to wonder at the game:
Sweet *Iupiter*, if ere I pleasde thine eye,
Or seemed faire walde in with Egles wings,
Grace my immortall beautie with this boone,
And I will spend my time in thy bright armes.

Iup. What ist sweet wagge I should deny thy youth?
Whose face reflects such pleasure to mine eyes,
As I exhal'd with thy fire darting beames,
Haue oft driuen backe the horses of the night.
When as they would haue hal'd thee from my sight:
Sit on my knee, and call for thy content,
Controule proud Fate, and cut the thred of time,
Why are not all the Gods at thy commaund,
And heauen and earth the bounds of thy delight?
Vulcan shall daunce to make thee laughing sport,

4

And my nine Daughters sing when thou art sad,
From *Iunos* bird Ile pluck her spotted pride,
To make thee fannes wherewith to coole thy face,
And *Venus* Swannes shall shed their siluer downe,
To sweeten out the slumbers of thy bed:
Hermes no more shall shew the world his wings,
If that thy fancie in his feathers dwell,
But as this one Ile teare them all from him,
Doe thou but say their colour pleaseth me:
Hold here my little loue these linked gems,
My *Iuno* ware vpon her marriage day,
Put thou about thy necke my owne sweet heart,
And tricke thy armes and shoulders with my theft.

Gan. I would haue a iewell for mine eare,
And a fine brouch to put in my hat,
And then Ile hugge with you an hundred times.
Iup. And shall haue *Ganimed*, if thou wilt be my loue.

Enter Venus.

Venus. I this is it, you can sit toying there,
And playing with that female wanton boy,
Whiles my *Æneas* wanders on the Seas,
And rests a pray to euery billowes pride.
Iuno, false *Iuno* in her Chariots pompe,
Drawne through the heauens by Steedes of *Boreas* brood,
Made *Hebe* to direct her ayrie wheeles
Into the windie countrie of the clowdes,
Where finding *Æolus* intrencht with stormes,
And guarded with a thousand grislie ghosts,
She humbly did beseech him for our bane,
And charg'd him drowne my sonne with all his traine.
Then gan the windes breake ope their brazen doores,
And all *Æolia* to be vp in armes:
Poore *Troy* must now be sackt vpon the Sea,
And *Neptunes* waues be enuious men of warre,
Epeus horse to *Ætnas* hill transformd,
Prepared stands to wracke their woodden walles,
And *Æolus* like *Agamemnon* sounds
The surges, his fierce souldiers to the spoyle:
See how the night *Ulysses*-like comes forth,
And intercepts the day as *Dolon* erst:
Ay me! the Starres supprisde like *Rhesus* Steedes,
Are drawne by darknes forth *Astræus* tents.

What shall I doe to saue thee my sweet boy?
When as the waues doe threat our Chrystall world,
And *Proteus* raising hils of flouds on high,
Entends ere long to sport him in the skie.
False *Iupiter*, rewardst thou vertue so?
What? is not pietie exempt from woe?
Then dye *Æneas* in thine innocence,
Since that religion hath no recompence.

Iup. Content thee *Cytherea* in thy care,
Since thy *Æneas* wandring fate is firme,
Whose wearie lims shall shortly make repose,
In those faire walles I promist him of yore:
But first in bloud must his good fortune bud,
Before he be the Lord of *Turnus* towne,
Or force her smile that hetherto hath frownd:
Three winters shall he with the Rutiles warre,
And in the end subdue them with his sword,
And full three Sommers likewise shall he waste,
In mannaging those fierce barbarian mindes:
Which once performd, poore *Troy* so long supprest,
From forth her ashes shall aduance her head,
And flourish once againe that erst was dead:
But bright *Ascanius* beauties better worke,
Who with the Sunne deuides one radiant shape,
Shall build his throne amidst those starrie towers,
That earth-borne *Atlas* groning vnderprops:
No bounds but heauen shall bound his Emperie,
Whose azured gates enchased with his name,
Shall make the morning halt her gray vprise,
To feede her eyes with his engrauen fame.
Thus in stoute *Hectors* race three hundred yeares,
The Romane Scepter royall shall remaine,
Till that a Princesse priest conceau'd by *Mars*,
Shall yeeld to dignitie a dubble birth,
Who will eternish *Troy* in their attempts.

Venus. How may I credite these thy flattering termes,
When yet both sea and sands beset their ships,
And *Phoebus* as in stygian pooles, refraines
To taint his tresses in the Tyrrhen maine?

Iup. I will take order for that presently:
Hermes awake, and haste to *Neptunes* realme,
Whereas the Wind-god warring now with Fate,

Besiege the ofspring of our kingly loynes,
Charge him from me to turne his stormie powers,
And fetter them in *Vulcans* sturdie brasse,
That durst thus proudly wrong our kinsmans peace.
Venus farewell, thy sonne shall be our care:
Come *Ganimed*, we must about this geare.

Exeunt Iupiter cum Ganimed.

Venus. Disquiet Seas lay downe your swelling lookes,
And court *Æneas* with your calmie cheere,
Whose beautious burden well might make you proude,
Had not the heauens conceau'd with hel-borne clowdes,
Vaild his resplendant glorie from your view,
For my sake pitie him *Oceanus*,
That erst-while issued from thy watrie loynes,
And had my being from thy bubling froth:
Triton I know hath fild his trumpe with *Troy*,
And therefore will take pitie on his toyle,
And call both *Thetis* and *Cimodoœ*,
To succour him in this extremitie.

Enter Æneas with Ascanius, with one or two more.

What? doe I see my sonne now come on shoare:
Venus, how art thou compast with content,
The while thine eyes attract their sought for ioyes:
Great *Iupiter*, still honourd maist thou be,
For this so friendly ayde in time of neede.
Here in this bush disguised will I stand,
Whiles my *Æneas* spends himselfe in plaints,
And heauen and earth with his vnrest acquaints.

Æn. You sonnes of care, companions of my course,
Priams misfortune followes vs by sea,
And *Helens* rape doth haunt thee at the heeles.
How many dangers haue we ouer past?
Both barking *Scilla*, and the sounding Rocks,
The *Cyclops* shelues, and grim *Ceranias* seate
Haue you oregone, and yet remaine aliue!
Pluck vp your hearts, since fate still rests our friend,
And chaunging heauens may those good daies returne,
Which *Pergama* did vaunt in all her pride.

Acha. Braue Prince of *Troy*, thou onely art our God,

That by thy vertues freest vs from annoy,
And makes our hopes suruiue to cunning ioyes:
Doe thou but smile, and clowdie heauen will cleare,
Whose night and day descendeth from thy browes:
Though we be now in extreame miserie,
And rest the map of weatherbeaten woe:
Yet shall the aged Sunne shed forth his aire,
To make vs liue vnto our former heate,
And euery beast the forrest doth send forth,
Bequeath her young ones to our scanted foode.

Asca. Father I faint, good father giue me meate.

Æn. Alas sweet boy, thou must be still a while,
Till we haue fire to dresse the meate we kild:
Gentle *Achates*, reach the Tinder boxe,
That we may make a fire to warme vs with,
And rost our new found victuals on this shoare.

Venus. See what strange arts necessitie findes out,
How neere my sweet *Æneas* art thou driuen?

Æn. Hold, take this candle and goe light a fire,
You shall haue leaues and windfall bowes enow
Neere to these woods, to rost your meate withall:
Ascanius, goe and drie thy drenched lims,
Whiles I with my *Achates* roaue abroad,
To know what coast the winde hath driuen vs on,
Or whether men or beasts inhabite it.

Acha. The ayre is pleasant, and the soyle most fit
For Cities, and societies supports:
Yet much I maruell that I cannot finde,
No steps of men imprinted in the earth.

Venus. Now is the time for me to play my part:
Hoe yong men, saw you as you came
Any of all my Sisters wandring here?
Hauing a quiuer girded to her side,
And cloathed in a spotted Leopards skin.

Æn. I neither saw nor heard of any such:
But what may I faire Virgin call your name?
Whose lookes set forth no mortall forme to view,
Nor speech bewraies ought humaine in thy birth,

8

Thou art a Goddesse that delud'st our eyes,
And shrowdes thy beautie in this borrowd shape;
But whether thou the Sunnes bright Sister be,
Or one of chast *Dianas* fellow Nimphs,
Liue happie in the height of all content,
And lighten our extreames with this one boone,
As to instruct vs vnder what good heauen
We breathe as now, and what this world is calde,
On which by tempests furie we are cast,
Tell vs, O tell vs that are ignorant,
And this right hand shall make thy Altars crack
With mountaine heapes of milke white Sacrifize.

Venus. Such honour, stranger, doe I not affect:
It is the vse for Turen maides to weare
Their bowe and quiuer in this modest sort,
And suite themselues in purple for the nonce,
That they may trip more lightly ore the lawndes,
And ouertake the tusked Bore in chase.
But for the land whereof thou doest enquire,
It is the punick kingdome rich and strong,
Adioyning on *Agenors* stately towne,
The kingly seate of Southerne *Libia*,
Whereas Sidonian *Dido* rules as Queene.
But what are you that aske of me these things?
Whence may you come, or whither will you goe?

Æn. Of *Troy* am I, *Æneas* is my name,
Who driuen by warre from forth my natiue world,
Put sailes to sea to seeke out *Italy*;
And my diuine descent from sceptred *Ioue*,
With twise twelue Phrigian ships I plowed the deepe,
And made that way my mother *Venus* led:
But of them all scarce seuen doe anchor safe,
And they so wrackt and weltred by the waues,
As euery tide tilts twixt their oken sides:
And all of them vnburdened of their loade,
Are ballassed with billowes watrie weight.
But haples I, God wot, poore and vnknowne,
Doe trace these Libian deserts all despisde,
Exild forth *Europe* and wide *Asia* both,
And haue not any couerture but heauen.

Venus. Fortune hath fauord thee what ere thou be,
In sending thee vnto this curteous Coast:

A Gods name on and hast thee to the Court,
Where *Dido* will receiue ye with her smiles:
And for thy ships which thou supposest lost,
Not one of them hath perisht in the storme,
But are ariued safe not farre from hence:
And so I leaue thee to thy fortunes lot,
Wishing good lucke vnto thy wandring steps. *Exit.*

Æn. Achates, tis my mother that is fled,
I know her by the mouings of her feete:
Stay gentle *Venus*, flye not from thy sonne,
Too cruell, why wilt thou forsake me thus?
Or in these shades deceiu'st mine eye so oft?
Why talke we not together hand in hand?
And tell our griefes in more familiar termes:
But thou art gone and leau'st me here alone,
To dull the ayre with my discoursiue moane. *Exit.*

Enter Illioneus, and Cloanthes.

Illio. Follow ye Troians, follow this braue Lord,
And plaine to him the summe of your distresse.

Iar. Why, what are you, or wherefore doe you sewe?

Illio. Wretches of *Troy*, enuied of the windes,
That craue such fauour at your honors feete,
As poore distressed miserie may pleade:
Saue, saue, O saue our ships from cruell fire,
That doe complaine the wounds of thousand waues,
And spare our liues whom euery spite pursues.
We come not we to wrong your Libian Gods,
Or steale your houshold lares from their shrines:
Our hands are not prepar'd to lawles spoyle,
Nor armed to offend in any kind:
Such force is farre from our vnweaponed thoughts,
Whose fading weale of victorie forsooke,
Forbids all hope to harbour neere our hearts.

Iar. But tell me Troians, Troians if you be,
Vnto what fruitfull quarters were ye bound,
Before that *Boreas* buckled with your sailes?

Cloan. There is a place *Hesperia* term'd by vs,
An ancient Empire, famoused for armes,

10

And fertile in faire *Ceres* furrowed wealth,
Which now we call *Italia* of his name,
That in such peace long time did rule the same:
Thither made we,
When suddenly gloomie *Orion* rose,
And led our ships into the shallow sands,
Whereas the Southerne winde with brackish breath,
Disperst them all amongst the wrackfull Rockes:
From thence a fewe of vs escapt to land,
The rest we feare are foulded in the flouds.

Iar. Braue men at armes, abandon fruitles feares,
Since Carthage knowes to entertaine distresse.

Serg. I but the barbarous sort doe threat our ships,
And will not let vs lodge vpon the sands:
In multitudes they swarme vnto the shoare,
And from the first earth interdict our feete.

Iar. My selfe will see they shall not trouble ye,
Your men and you shall banquet in our Court,
And euery Troian be as welcome here,
As *Iupiter* to sillie *Vausis* house:
Come in with me, Ile bring you to my Queene,
Who shall confirme my words with further deedes.

Serg. Thankes gentle Lord for such vnlookt for grace,
Might we but once more see *Æneas* face,
Then would we hope to quite such friendly turnes,
As shall surpasse the wonder of our speech.

Actus 2

Enter Æneas, Achates, and Ascanius.

Æn. Where am I now? these should be Carthage walles.

Acha. Why stands my sweete *Æneas* thus amazde?

Æn. O my *Achates*, Theban *Niobe*,
Who for her sonnes death wept out life and breath,
And drie with griefe was turnd into a stone,
Had not such passions in her head as I.
Me thinkes that towne there should be *Troy*, yon *Idas* hill,
There *Zanthus* streame, because here's *Priamus*,
And when I know it is not, then I dye.

Ach. And in this humor is *Achates* to,
I cannot choose but fall vpon my knees,
And kisse his hand: O where is *Hecuba*,
Here she was wont to sit, but sauing ayre
Is nothing here, and what is this but stone?

Æn. O yet this stone doth make *Æneas* weepe,
And would my prayers (as *Pigmalions* did)
Could giue it life, that vnder his conduct
We might saile backe to *Troy* and be reuengde
On these hard harted Grecians; which reioyce
That nothing now is left of *Priamus*:
O *Priamus* is left and this is he,
Come, come abourd, pursue the hatefull Greekes.

Acha. What means *Æneas*?

Æn. Achates though mine eyes say this is stone,
Yet thinkes my minde that this is *Priamus*:
And when my grieued heart sighes and sayes no,
Then would it leape out to giue *Priam* life:
O were I not at all so thou mightst be.
Achates, see King *Priam* wags his hand,
He is aliue, *Troy* is not ouercome.

Ach. Thy mind *Æneas* that would haue it so

Deludes thy eye sight, *Priamus* is dead.

Æn. Ah *Troy* is sackt, and *Priamus* is dead,
And why should poore *Æneas* be aliue?

Asca. Sweete father leaue to weepe, this is not he:
For were it *Priam* he would smile on me.

Acha. Æneas see here come the Citizens,
Leaue to lament lest they laugh at our feares.

Enter Cloanthus, Sergestus, Illioneus.

Æn. Lords of this towne, or whatsoeuer stile
Belongs vnto your name, vouchsafe of ruth
To tell vs who inhabits this faire towne,
What kind of people, and who gouernes them:
For we are strangers driuen on this shore,
And scarcely know within what Clime we are.

Illio. I heare *Æneas* voyce, but see him not,
For none of these can be our Generall.

Acha. Like *Illioneus* speakes this Noble man,
But *Illioneus* goes not in such robes.

Serg. You are *Achates*, or I deciu'd.

Acha. Æneas see *Sergestus* or his ghost.

Illio. He meanes *Æneas*, let vs kisse his feete.

Cloan. It is our Captaine, see *Ascanius.*

Serg. Liue long *Æneas* and *Ascanius.*

Æn. Achates, speake, for I am ouerioyed.

Acha. O *Illioneus*, art thou yet aliue?

Illio. Blest be the time I see *Achates* face.

Cloan. Why turnes *Æneas* from his trustie friends?

Æn. Sergestus, Illioneus and the rest,

Your sight amazde me, O what destinies
Haue brought my sweete companions in such plight?
O tell me, for I long to be resolu'd.

Illio. Louely *Æneas*, these are Carthage walles,
And here Queene *Dido* weares th'imperiall Crowne,
Who for *Troyes* sake hath entertaind vs all,
And clad vs in these wealthie robes we weare.
Oft hath she askt vs vnder whom we seru'd,
And when we told her she would weepe for griefe,
Thinking the sea had swallowed vp thy ships,
And now she sees thee how will she reioyce?

Serg. See where her seruitors passe through the hall
Bearing a banket, *Dido* is not farre.

Illio. Looke where she comes: *Æneas* viewd her well.

Æn. Well may I view her, but she sees not me.

Enter Dido and her traine.

Dido. What stranger art thou that doest eye me thus?

Æn. Sometime I was a Troian mightie Queene:
But *Troy* is not, what shall I say I am?

Illio. Renowmed *Dido*, tis our Generall: warlike *Æneas*.

Dido. Warlike *Æneas*, and in these base robes?
Goe fetch the garment which *Sicheus* ware:
Braue Prince, welcome to Carthage and to me,
Both happie that *Æneas* is our guest:
Sit in this chaire and banquet with a Queene,
Æneas is *Æneas*, were he clad
In weedes as bad as euer *Irus* ware.

Æn. This is no seate for one thats comfortles,
May it please your grace to let *Æneas* waite:
For though my birth be great, my fortunes meane,
Too meane to be companion to a Queene.

Dido. Thy fortune may be greater then thy birth,
Sit downe *Æneas*, sit in *Didos* place,
And if this be thy sonne as I suppose,

14

Here let him sit, be merrie louely child.

Æn. This place beseemes me not, O pardon me.

Dido. Ile haue it so, *Æneas* be content.

Asca. Madame, you shall be my mother.

Dido. And so I will sweete child: be merrie man,
Heres to thy better fortune and good starres.

Æn. In all humilitie I thanke your grace.

Dido. Remember who thou art, speake like thy selfe,
Humilitie belongs to common groomes.

Æn. And who so miserable as *Æneas* is?

Dido. Lyes it in *Didos* hands to make thee blest,
Then be assured thou art not miserable.

Æn. O *Priamus*, O *Troy*, oh *Hecuba*!

Dido. May I entreate thee to discourse at large,
And truely to how *Troy* was ouercome:
For many tales goe of that Cities fall,
And scarcely doe agree vpon one poynt:
Some say *Antenor* did betray the towne,
Others report twas *Sinons* periurie:
But all in this that *Troy* is ouercome,
And *Priam* dead, yet how we heare no newes.

Æn. A wofull tale bids *Dido* to vnfould,
Whose memorie like pale deaths stony mace,
Beates forth my senses from this troubled soule,
And makes *Æneas* sinke at *Didos* feete.

Dido. What faints *Æneas* to remember *Troy*?
In whose defence he fought so valiantly:
Looke vp and speake.

Æn. Then speake *Æneas* with *Achilles* tongue,
And *Dido* and you Carthaginian Peeres
Heare me, but yet with *Mirmidons* harsh eares,
Daily inur'd to broyles and Massacres,

Lest you be mou'd too much with my sad tale.
The Grecian souldiers tired with ten yeares warre;
Began to crye, let vs vnto our ships,
Troy is inuincible, why stay we here?
With whose outcryes *Atrides* being apal'd,
Summoned the Captaines to his princely tent,
Who looking on the scarres we Troians gaue,
Seeing the number of their men decreast,
And the remainder weake and out of heart,
Gaue vp their voyces to dislodge the Campe,
And so in troopes all marcht to *Tenedos*:
Where when they came, *Vlysses* on the sand
Assayd with honey words to turne them backe:
And as he spoke to further his entent,
The windes did driue huge billowes to the shoare,
And heauen was darkned with tempestuous clowdes:
Then he alleag'd the Gods would haue them stay,
And prophecied *Troy* should be ouercome:
And therewithall he calde false *Sinon* forth,
A man compact of craft and periurie,
Whose ticing tongue was made of *Hermes* pipe,
To force an hundred watchfull eyes to sleepe:
And him *Epeus* hauing made the horse,
With sacrificing wreathes vpon his head,
Vlysses sent to our vnhappie towne:
Who groueling in the mire of *Zanthus* bankes,
His hands bound at his back, and both his eyes
Turnd vp to heauen as one resolu'd to dye,
Our Phrigian shepherd haled within the gates,
And brought vnto the Court of *Priamus*:
To whom he vsed action so pitifull,
Lookes so remorcefull, vowes so forcible,
As therewithall the old man ouercome,
Kist him, imbrast him, and vnloosde his bands,
And then, O *Dido* pardon me.

Dido. Nay leaue not here, resolue me of the rest.

Æn. O th'inchaunting words of that base slaue,
Made him to thinke *Epeus* pine-tree Horse
A sacrifize t'appease *Mineruas* wrath:
The rather for that one *Laocoon*
Breaking a speare vpon his hollow breast,
Was with two winged Serpents stung to death.
Whereat agast, we were commanded straight

16

With reuerence to draw it into *Troy*.
In which vnhappie worke was I employd,
These hands did helpe to hale it to the gates,
Through which it could not enter twas so huge.
O had it neuer entred, *Troy* had stood.
But *Priamus* impatient of delay,
Inforst a wide breach in that rampierd wall,
Which thousand battering Rams could neuer pierce,
And so came in this fatall instrument:
At whose accursed feete as ouerioyed,
We banquetted till ouercome with wine,
Some surfetted, and others soundly slept.
Which *Sinon* viewing, causde the Greekish spyes
To hast to *Tenedos* and tell the Campe:
Then he vnlockt the Horse, and suddenly
From out his entrailes, *Neoptolemus*
Setting his speare vpon the ground, leapt forth,
And after him a thousand Grecians more,
In whose sterne faces shin'd the quenchles fire,
That after burnt the pride of *Asia*.
By this the Campe was come vnto the walles,
And through the breach did march into the streetes,
Where meeting with the rest, kill kill they cryed.
Frighted with this confused noyse, I rose,
And looking from a turret, might behold
Yong infants swimming in their parents bloud,
Headles carkasses piled vp in heapes,
Virgins halfe dead dragged by their golden haire,
And with maine force flung on a ring of pikes,
Old men with swords thrust through their aged sides,
Kneeling for mercie to a Greekish lad,
Who with steele Pol-axes dasht out their braines.
Then buckled I mine armour, drew my sword,
And thinking to goe downe, came *Hectors* ghost
With ashie visage, blewish, sulphure eyes,
His armes torne from his shoulders, and his breast
Furrowd with wounds, and that which made me weepe,
Thongs at his heeles, by which *Achilles* horse
Drew him in triumph through the Greekish Campe,
Burst from the earth, crying, *Æneas* flye,
Troy is a fire, the Grecians haue the towne,

Dido. O *Hector* who weepes not to heare thy name?

Æn. Yet flung I forth, and desperate of my life,

17

Ran in the thickest throngs, and with this sword
Sent many of their sauadge ghosts to hell.
At last came *Pirrhus* fell and full of ire.
His harnesse dropping bloud, and on his speare
The mangled head of *Priams* yongest sonne,
And after him his band of Mirmidons,
With balles of wilde fire in their murdering pawes,
Which made the funerall flame that burnt faire *Troy*:
All which hemd me about, crying, this is he.

Dido. Ah, how could poore *Æneas* scape their hands?

Æn. My mother *Venus* iealous of my health,
Conuaid me from their crooked nets and bands:
So I escapt the furious *Pirrhus* wrath:
Who then ran to the pallace of the King,
And at *Ioues* Altar finding *Priamus*,
About whose withered necke hung *Hecuba*,
Foulding his hand in hers, and ioyntly both
Beating their breasts and falling on the ground,
He with his faulchions poynt raisde vp at once,
And with *Megeras* eyes stared in their face,
Threatning a thousand deaths at euery glaunce.
To whom the aged King thus trembling spoke:
Achilles sonne, remember what I was,
Father of fiftie sonnes, but they are slaine,
Lord of my fortune, but my fortunes turnd,
King of this Citie, but my *Troy* is fired,
And now am neither father, Lord, nor King:
Yet who so wretched but desires to liue?
O let me liue, great *Neoptolemus*,
Not mou'd at all, but smiling at his teares,
This butcher whil'st his hands were yet held vp,
Treading vpon his breast, strooke off his hands.

Dido. O end *Æneas*, I can heare no more.

Æn. At which the franticke Queene leapt on his face,
And in his eyelids hanging by the nayles,
A little while prolong'd her husbands life:
At last the souldiers puld her by the heeles,
And swong her howling in the emptie ayre,
Which sent an eccho to the wounded King:
Whereat he lifted vp his bedred lims,
And would haue grappeld with *Achilles* sonne,

Forgetting both his want of strength and hands,
Which he disdaining whiskt his sword about,
And with the wound thereof the King fell downe:
Then from the nauell to the throat at once,
He ript old *Priam*: at whose latter gaspe
Ioues marble statue gan to bend the brow,
As lothing *Pirrhus* for this wicked act:
Yet he vndaunted tooke his fathers flagge,
And dipt it in the old Kings chill cold bloud,
And then in triumph ran into the streetes,
Through which he could not passe for slaughtred men:
So leaning on his sword he stood stone still,
Viewing the fire wherewith rich *Ilion* burnt.
By this I got my father on my backe,
This yong boy in mine armes, and by the hand
Led faire *Creusa* my beloued wife,
When thou *Achates* with thy sword mad'st way,
And we were round inuiron'd with the Greekes:
O there I lost my wife: and had not we
Fought manfully, I had not told this tale:
Yet manhood would not serue, of force we fled,
And as we went vnto our ships, thou knowest
We sawe *Cassandra* sprauling in the streetes,
Whom *Aiax* rauisht in *Dianas* Fawne,
Her cheekes swolne with sighes, her haire all rent,
Whom I tooke vp to beare vnto our ships;
But suddenly the Grecians followed vs,
And I alas, was forst to let her lye.
Then got we to our ships, and being abourd,
Polixena cryed out, *Æneas* stay,
The Greekes pursue me, stay and take me in.
Moued with her voyce, I lept into the sea,
Thinking to beare her on my backe abourd:
For all our ships were launcht into the deepe,
And as I swomme, she standing on the shoare,
Was by the cruell Mirmidons surprizd,
And after by that *Pirrhus* sacrifizde.

Dido. I dye with melting ruth, *Æneas* leaue.

Anna. O what became of aged *Hecuba*?

Iar. How got *Æneas* to the fleete againe?

Dido. But how scapt *Helen*, she that causde this warre?

19

Æn. *Achates* speake, sorrow hath tired me quite.

Acha. What happened to the Queene we cannot shewe,
We heare they led her captiue into Greece,
As for *Æneas* he swomme quickly backe,
And *Helena* betraied *Diiphobus*
Her Louer, after *Alexander* dyed,
And so was reconcil'd to *Menelaus.*

Dido. O had that ticing strumpet nere been borne:
Troian, thy ruthfull tale hath made me sad:
Come let vs thinke vpon some pleasing sport,
To rid me from these melancholly thoughts.

Exeunt omnes.

Enter Venus at another doore, and takes Ascanius by the sleeve.

Venus. Faire child stay thou with *Didos* waiting maide,
Ile giue thee Sugar-almonds, sweete Conserues,
A siluer girdle, and a golden purse,
And this yong Prince shall be thy playfellow.

Asca. Are you Queene *Didos* sonne?

Cupid. I, and my mother gaue me this fine bow.

Asca. Shall I haue such a quiuer and a bow?

Venus. Such bow, such quiuer, and such golden shafts,
Will *Dido* giue to sweete *Ascanius*:
For *Didos* sake I take thee in my armes,
And sticke these spangled feathers in thy hat,
Eate Comfites in mine armes, and I will sing.
Now is he fast asleepe, and in this groue
Amongst greene brakes Ile lay *Ascanius*,
And strewe him with sweete smelling Violets,
Blushing Roses, purple *Hyacinthe*:
These milke white Doues shall be his Centronels:
Who if that any seeke to doe him hurt,
Will quickly flye to *Citheidas* fist.
Now *Cupid* turne thee to *Ascanius* shape,
And goe to *Dido* who in stead of him
Will set thee on her lap and play with thee:

Then touch her white breast with this arrow head,
That she may dote vpon *Æneas* loue:
And by that meanes repaire his broken ships,
Victuall his Souldiers, giue him wealthie gifts,
And he at last depart to *Italy*,
Or els in *Carthage* make his kingly throne.

Cupid. I will faire mother, and so play my part,
As euery touch shall wound Queene *Didos* heart.

Venus. Sleepe my sweete nephew in these cooling shades,
Free from the murmure of these running streames,
The crye of beasts, the ratling of the windes,
Or whisking of these leaues, all shall be still,
And nothing interrupt thy quiet sleepe,
Till I returne and take thee hence againe. *Exit.*

Actus 3.

Scena I.

Enter Cupid solus.

Cupid. Now *Cupid* cause the Carthaginian Queene,
To be inamourd of thy brothers lookes,
Conuey this golden arrowe in thy sleeue,
Lest she imagine thou art *Venus* sonne:
And when she strokes thee softly on the head,
Then shall I touch her breast and conquer her.

Enter Iarbus, Anna, and Dido.

Iar. How long faire *Dido* shall I pine for thee?
Tis not enough that thou doest graunt me loue,
But that I may enioy what I desire:
That loue is childish which consists in words.

Dido. Iarbus, know that thou of all my wooers
(And yet haue I had many mightier Kings)
Hast had the greatest fauours I could giue:
I feare me *Dido* hath been counted light,
In being too familiar with *Iarbus*:
Albeit the Gods doe know no wanton thought
Had euer residence in *Didos* breast.

Iar. But *Dido* is the fauour I request.

Dido. Feare not *Iarbus, Dido* may be thine.

Anna. Looke sister how *Æneas* little sonne
Playes with your garments and imbraceth you.

Cupid. No *Dido* will not take me in her armes,
I shall not be her sonne, she loues me not.

Dido. Weepe not sweet boy, thou shalt be *Didos* sonne,
Sit in my lap and let me heare thee sing.
No more my child, now talke another while,
And tell me where learnst thou this pretie song?

Cupid. My cosin *Helen* taught it me in *Troy.*

Dido. How louely is *Ascanius* when he smiles?

Cupid. Will *Dido* let me hang about her necke?

Dido. I wagge, and giue thee leaue to kisse her to.

Cupid. What will you giue me? now Ile haue this Fanne.

Dido. Take it *Ascanius*, for thy fathers sake.

Iar. Come *Dido*, leaue *Ascanius*, let vs walke.

Dido. Goe thou away, *Ascanius* shall stay.

Iar. Vngentle Queene, is this thy loue to me?

Dido. O stay *Iarbus*, and Ile goe with thee.

Cupid. And if my mother goe, Ile follow her.

Dido. Why staiest thou here? thou art no loue of mine?

Iar. *Iarbus* dye, seeing she abandons thee.

Dido. No, liue *Iarbus*, what hast thou deseru'd,
That I should say thou art no loue of mine?
Something thou hast deseru'd, away I say,
Depart from *Carthage*, come not in my sight.

Iar. Am I not King of rich *Getulia*?

Dido. *Iarbus* pardon me, and stay a while.

Cupid. Mother, looke here.

Dido. What telst thou me of rich *Getulia*?
Am not I Queene of *Libia*? then depart.

Iar. I goe to feed the humour of my Loue,
Yet not from *Carthage* for a thousand worlds.

Dido. *Iarbus.*

23

Iar. Doth *Dido* call me backe?

Dido. No, but I charge thee neuer looke on me.

Iar. Then pull out both mine eyes, or let me dye. *Exit Iarb.*

Anna. Wherefore doth *Dido* bid *Iarbus* goe?

Dido. Because his lothsome sight offends mine eye,
And in my thoughts is shrin'd another loue:
O *Anna*, didst thou know how sweet loue were,
Full soone wouldst thou abiure this single life.

Anna. Poore soule I know too well the sower of loue,
O that *Iarbus* could but fancie me.

Dido. Is not *Æneas* faire and beautifull?

Anna. Yes, and *Iarbus* foule and fauourles.

Dido. Is he not eloquent in all his speech?

Anna. Yes, and *Iarbus* rude and rusticall.

Dido. Name not *Iarbus*, but sweete *Anna* say,
Is not *Æneas* worthie *Didos* loue?

Anna. O sister, were you Empresse of the world,
Æneas well deserues to be your loue,
So lovely is he that where ere he goes,
The people swarme to gaze him in the face.

Dido. But tell them none shall gaze on him but I,
Lest their grosse eye-beames taint my louers cheekes:
Anna, good sister *Anna* goe for him,
Lest with these sweete thoughts I melt cleane away.

Anna. Then sister youle abiure *Iarbus* loue?

Dido. Yet must I heare that lothsome name againe?
Runne for *Æneas*, or Ile flye to him. *Exit Anna.*

Cupid. You shall not hurt my father when he comes.

Dido. No, for thy sake Ile loue thy father well.
O dull conceipted *Dido*, that till now
Didst neuer thinke *Æneas* beautifull:
But now for quittance of this ouersight,
Ile make me bracelets of his golden haire,
His glistering eyes shall be my looking glasse,
His lips an altar, where Ile offer vp
As many kisses as the Sea hath sands,
In stead of musicke I will heare him speake,
His lookes shall be my only Librarie,
And thou *Æneas, Didos* treasurie,
In whose faire bosome I will locke more wealth,
Then twentie thousand Indiaes can affoord:
O here he comes, loue, loue, giue *Dido* leaue
To be more modest then her thoughts admit,
Lest I be made a wonder to the world.
Achates, how doth *Carthage* please your Lord?

Acha. That will *Æneas* shewe your maiestie.

Dido. Æneas art thou there?

Æn. I vnderstand your highnesse sent for me.

Dido. No, but now thou art here, tell me in sooth,
In what might *Dido* highly pleasure thee.

Æn. So much haue I receiu'd at *Didos* hands,
As without blushing I can aske no more:
Yet Queene of *Affricke*, are my ships vnrigd,
My Sailes all rent in sunder with the winde,
My Oares broken, and my Tackling lost,
Yea all my Nauie split with Rockes and Shelfes:
Nor Sterne nor Anchor haue our maimed Fleete,
Our Masts the furious windes strooke ouer bourd:
Which piteous wants if *Dido* will supplie,
We will account her author of our liues.

Dido. Æneas, Ile repaire thy Troian ships,
Conditionally that thou wilt stay with me,
And let *Achates* saile to *Italy*:
Ile giue thee tackling made of riueld gold,
Wound on the barkes of odoriferous trees,
Oares of massie Iuorie full of holes,
Through which the water shall delight to play:

Thy Anchors shall be hewed from Christall Rockes,
Which if thou lose shall shine aboue the waues;
The Masts whereon thy swelling sailes shall hang,
Hollow Pyramides of siluer plate:
The sailes of foulded Lawne, where shall be wrought
The warres of *Troy*, but not *Troyes* ouerthrow:
For ballace, emptie *Didos* treasurie,
Take what ye will, but leaue *Æneas* here.
Achates, thou shalt be so meanly clad,
As Seaborne Nymphes shall swarme about thy ships,
And wanton Mermaides court thee with sweete songs,
Flinging in fauours of more soueraigne worth,
Then *Thetis* hangs about *Apolloes* necke,
So that *Æneas* may but stay with me.

Æn. Wherefore would *Dido* haue *Æneas* stay?

Dido. To warre against my bordering enemies:
Æneas, thinke not *Dido* is in loue:
For if that any man could conquer me,
I had been wedded ere *Æneas* came:
See where the pictures of my suiters hang,
And are not these as faire as faire may be?

Acha. I saw this man at *Troy* ere *Troy* was sackt.

Æn. I this in *Greece* when *Paris* stole faire *Helen.*

Illio. This man and I were at *Olympus* games.

Serg. I know this face, he is a Persian borne,
I traueld with him to *Ætolia.*

Cloan. And I in *Athens* with this gentleman,
Vnlesse I be deceiu'd disputed once.

Dido. But speake *Æneas*, know you none of these?

Æn. No Madame, but it seemes that these are Kings.

Dido. All these and others which I neuer sawe,
Haue been most vrgent suiters for my loue,
Some came in person, others sent their Legats:
Yet none obtaind me, I am free from all,
And yet God knowes intangled vnto one.

This was an Orator, and thought by words
To compasse me, but yet he was deceiu'd:
And this a Spartan Courtier vaine and wilde,
But his fantastick humours pleasde not me:
This was *Alcion*, a Musition,
But playd he nere so sweet, I let him goe:
This was the wealthie King of *Thessaly*,
But I had gold enough and cast him off:
This *Meleagers* sonne, a warlike Prince,
But weapons gree not with my tender yeares:
The rest are such as all the world well knowes,
Yet how I sweare by heauen and him I loue,
I was as farre from loue, as they from hate.

Æn. O happie shall he be whom *Dido* loues.

Dido. Then neuer say that thou art miserable,
Because it may be thou shalt be my loue:
Yet boast not of it, for I loue thee not,
And yet I hate thee not: O if I speake
I shall betray my selfe: *Æneas* speake,
We two will goe a hunting in the woods,
But not so much for thee, thou art but one,
As for *Achates*, and his followers.   *Exeunt.*

Enter Iuno to Ascanius asleepe.

Iuno. Here lyes my hate, *Æneas* cursed brat,
The boy wherein false destinie delights,
The heire of furie, the fauorite of the face,
That vgly impe that shall outweare my wrath,
And wrong my deitie with high disgrace:
But I will take another order now,
And race th'eternall Register of time:
Troy shall no more call him her second hope,
Nor *Venus* triumph in his tender youth:
For here in spight of heauen Ile murder him,
And feede infection with his left out life:
Say *Paris*, now shall *Venus* haue the ball?
Say vengeance, now shall her *Ascanius* dye.
O no God wot, I cannot watch my time,
Nor quit good turnes with double fee downe told:
Tut, I am simple without made to hurt,
And haue no gall at all to grieue my foes:
But lustfull *Ioue* and his adulterous child,

27

Shall finde it written on confusions front,
That onely *Iuno* rules in *Rhamnuse* towne.

Enter Venus.

Venus. What should this meane? my Doues are back returnd,
Who warne me of such daunger prest at hand,
To harme my sweete *Ascanius* louely life.
Iuno, my mortall foe, what make you here?
Auaunt old witch and trouble not my wits.

Iuno. Fie *Venus*, that such causeles words of wrath,
Should ere defile so faire a mouth as thine:
Are not we both sprong of celestiall rase,
And banquet as two Sisters with the Gods?
Why is it then displeasure should disioyne,
Whom kindred and acquaintance counites.

Venus. Out hatefull hag, thou wouldst haue slaine my sonne,
Had not my Doues discou'rd thy entent:
But I will teare thy eyes fro forth thy head,
And feast the birds with their bloud-shotten balles,
If thou but lay thy fingers on my boy.

Iuno. Is this then all the thankes that I shall haue,
For sauing him from Snakes and Serpents stings,
That would haue kild him sleeping as he lay?
What though I was offended with thy sonne,
And wrought him mickle woe on sea and land,
When for the hate of Troian *Ganimed*,
That was aduanced by my *Hebes* shame,
And *Paris* iudgement of the heauenly ball,
I mustred all the windes vnto his wracke,
And vrg'd each Element to his annoy:
Yet now I doe repent me of his ruth,
And wish that I had neuer wrongd him so:
Bootles I sawe it was to warre with fate,
That hath so many vnresisted friends:
Wherefore I chaunge my counsell with the time,
And planted loue where enuie erst had sprong.

Venus. Sister of *Ioue*, if that thy loue be such,
As these thy protestations doe paint forth,
We two as friends one fortune will deuide:
Cupid shall lay his arrowes in thy lap,

And to a Scepter chaunge his golden shafts,
Fancie and modestie shall liue as mates,
And thy faire peacockes by my pigeons pearch:
Loue my *Æneas*, and desire is thine,
The day, the night, my Swannes, my sweetes are thine.

Iuno. More then melodious are these words to me,
That ouercioy my soule with their content:
Venus, sweete *Venus*, how may I deserue
Such amourous fauours at thy beautious hand?
But that thou maist more easilie perceiue,
How highly I doe prize this amitie,
Harke to a motion of eternall league,
Which I will make in quittance of thy loue:
Thy sonne thou knowest with *Dido* now remaines,
And feedes his eyes with fauours of her Court,
She likewise in admyring spends her time,
And cannot talke nor thinke of ought but him:
Why should not they then ioyne in marriage,
And bring forth mightie Kings to Carthage towne,
Whom casualtie of sea hath made such friends?
And *Venus*, let there be a match confirmd
Betwixt these two, whose loues are so alike,
And both our Deities conioynd in one,
Shall chaine felicitie vnto their throne.

Venus. Well could I like this reconcilements meanes,
But much I feare my sonne will nere consent,
Whose armed soule alreadie on the sea,
Darts forth her light to *Lauinias* shoare.

Iuno. Faire Queene of loue, I will deuorce these doubts,
And finde the way to wearie such fond thoughts:
This day they both a hunting forth will ride
Into these woods, adioyning to these walles,
When in the midst of all their gamesome sports,
Ile make the Clowdes dissolue their watrie workes,
And drench *Siluanus* dwellings with their shewers,
Then in one Caue the Queene and he shall meete,
And interchangeably discourse their thoughts,
Whose short conclusion will seale vp their hearts,
Vnto the purpose which we now propound.

Venus. Sister, I see you sauour of my wiles,
Be it as you will haue for this once,

29

Meane time, *Ascanius* shall be my charge,
Whom I will beare to *Ida* in mine armes,
And couch him in *Adonis* purple downe, *Exeunt.*

Enter Dido, Æneas, Anna, Iarbus, Achates, and followers.

Dido. Æneas, thinke not but I honor thee,
That thus in person goe with thee to hunt:
My princely robes thou seest are layd aside,
Whose glittering pompe *Dianas* shrowdes supplies,
All fellowes now disposde alike to sporte,
The woods are wide, and we haue store of game:
Faire Troian, hold my golden bowe awhile,
Vntill I gird my quiuer to my side:
Lords goe before, we two must talke alone.

Iar. Vngentle, can she wrong *Iarbus* so?
Ile dye before a stranger haue that grace:
We two will talke alone, what words be these?

Dido. What makes *Iarbus* here of all the rest?
We could haue gone without your companie.

Æn. But loue and duetie led him on perhaps,
To presse beyond acceptance to your sight.

Iar. Why man of *Troy*, doe I offend thine eyes?
Or art thou grieude thy betters presse so nye?

Dido. How now Getulian, are ye growne so braue,
To challenge vs with your comparisons?
Pesant, goe seeke companions like thy selfe,
And meddle not with any that I loue:
Æneas, be not moude at what he sayes,
For otherwhile he will be out of ioynt.

Iar. Women may wrong by priuiledge of loue:
But should that man of men (*Dido* except)
Haue taunted me in these opprobrious termes,
I would haue either drunke his dying bloud,
Or els I would haue giuen my life in gage?

Dido. Huntsmen, why pitch you not your toyles apace,
And rowse the light foote Deere from forth their laire.

Anna. Sister, see see *Ascanius* in his pompe,
Bearing his huntspeare brauely in his hand.

Dido. Yea little sonne, are you so forward now?

Asca. I mother, I shall one day be a man,
And better able vnto other armes,
Meane time these wanton weapons serue my warre,
Which I will breake betwixt a Lyons iawes.

Dido. What, darest thou looke a Lyon in the face?

Asca. I, and outface him to, doe what he can.

Anna. How like his father speaketh he in all?

Æn. And mought I liue to see him sacke rich *Thebes*,
And loade his speare with Grecian Princes heads,
Then would I wish me with *Anchises* Tombe,
And dead to honour that hath brought me vp.

Iar. And might I liue to see thee shipt away,
And hoyst aloft on *Neptunes* hideous hilles,
Then would I wish me in faire *Didos* armes,
And dead to scorne that hath pursued me so.

Æn. Stoute friend *Achates*, doest thou know this wood?

Acha. As I remember, here you shot the Deere,
That sau'd your famisht souldiers liues from death,
When first you set your foote vpon the shoare,
And here we met fair *Venus* virgine like,
Bearing her bowe and quiuer at her backe.

Æn. O how these irksome labours now delight,
And ouerioy my thoughts with their escape:
Who would not vndergoe all kind of toyle,
To be well stor'd with such a winters tale?

Dido. *Æneas*, leaue these dumpes and lets away,
Some to the mountaines, some vnto the soyle,
You to the vallies, thou vnto the house.

Exeunt omnes: manent.

Iar. I, this it is which wounds me to the death,
To see a Phrigian far fet to the sea,
Preferd before a man of maiestie:
O loue, O hate, O cruell womens hearts,
That imitate the Moone in euery chaunge,
And like the Planets euer loue to raunge:
What shall I doe thus wronged with disdaine?
Reuenge me on *Æneas*, or on her:
On her? fond man, that were to warre gainst heauen,
And with one shaft prouoke ten thousand darts:
This Troians end will be thy enuies aime,
Whose bloud will reconcile thee to content,
And make loue drunken with thy sweete desire:
But *Dido* that now holdeth him so deare,
Will dye with very tidings of his death:
But time will discontinue her content,
And mould her minde vnto newe fancies shapes:
O God of heauen, turne the hand of fate
Vnto that happie day of my delight,
And then, what then? *Iarbus* shall but loue:
So doth he now, though not with equall gaine,
That resteth in the riuall of thy paine,
Who nere will cease to soare till he be slaine. *Exit.*

The storme. Enter Æneas and Dido in the Caue at seuerall times.

Dido. Æneas.

Æn. Dido.

Dido. Tell me deare loue, how found you out this Caue?

Æn. By chance sweete Queene, as *Mars* and *Venus* met.

Dido. Why, that was in a net, where we are loose,
And yet I am not free, oh would I were.

Æn. Why, what is it that *Dido* may desire
And not obtaine, be it in humaine power?

Dido. The thing that I will dye before I aske,
And yet desire to haue before I dye.

Æn. It is not ought *Æneas* may achieue?

Dido. Æneas no, although his eyes doe pearce.

Æn. What, hath *Iarbus* angred her in ought?
And will she be auenged on his life?

Dido. Not angred me, except in angring thee.

Æn. Who then of all so cruell may he be,
That should detaine thy eye in his defects?

Dido. The man that I doe eye where ere I am,
Whose amorous face like *Pean* sparkles fire,
When as he buts his beames on *Floras* bed,
Prometheus hath put on *Cupids* shape,
And I must perish in his burning armes:
Æneas, O *Æneas*, quench these flames.

Æn. What ailes my Queene, is she falne sicke of late?

Dido. Not sicke my loue, but sicke, I must conceale
The torment, that it bootes me not reueale;
And yet Ile speake, and yet Ile hold my peace,
Doe shame her worst, I will disclose my griefe:
Æneas, thou art he, what did I say?
Something it was that now I haue forgot.

Æn. What meanes faire *Dido* by this doubtfull speech?

Dido. Nay, nothing, but *Æneas* loues me not.

Æn. *Æneas* thoughts dare not ascend so high
As *Didos* heart, which Monarkes might not scale.

Dido. It was because I sawe no King like thee,
Whose golden Crowne might ballance my content:
But now that I haue found what to effect,
I followe one that loueth fame for me,
And rather had seeme faire *Sirens* eyes,
Then to the Carthage Queene that dyes for him.

Æn. If that your maiestie can looke so lowe,
As my despised worths, that shun all praise,
With this my hand I giue to you my heart,
And vow by all the Gods of Hospitalitie,
By heauen and earth, and my faire brothers bowe,

By *Paphos*, *Capys*, and the purple Sea,
From whence my radiant mother did descend,
And by this Sword that saued me from the Greekes,
Neuer to leaue these newe vpreared walles,
Whiles *Dido* liues and rules in *Iunos* towne,
Neuer to like or loue any but her.

Dido. What more then delian musicke doe I heare,
That calles my soule from forth his liuing seate,
To moue vnto the measures of delight:
Kind clowdes that sent forth such a curteous storme,
As made disdaine to flye to fancies lap:
Stoute loue in mine armes make thy *Italy*,
Whose Crowne and kingdome rests at thy commande.
Sicheus, not *Æneas* be thou calde:
The King of *Carthage*, not *Anchises* sonne:
Hold, take these Iewels at thy Louers hand,
These golden bracelets, and this wedding ring,
Wherewith my husband woo'd me yet a maide,
And be thou king of *Libia*, by my guift.

Exeunt to the Caue.

Actus 4.

Scena 1.

Enter Achates, Ascanius, Iarbus, and Anna.

Acha. Did euer men see such a sudden storme?
Or day so cleere so suddenly orecast?

Iar. I thinke some fell Inchantresse dwelleth here,
That can call them forth when as she please,
And diue into blacke tempests treasurie,
When as she mcanes to maske the world with clowdes.

Anna. In all my life I neuer knew the like,
It haild, it snowde, it lightned all at once.

Acha. I thinke it was the diuels reuelling night,
There was such hurly burly in the heauens:
Doubtles *Apollos* Axeltree is crackt,
Or aged *Atlas* shoulder out of ioynt,
The motion was soouer violent.

Iar. In all this coyle, where haue ye left the Queene?

Asca. Nay, where is my warlike father, can you tell?

Anna. Behold where both of them come forth the Caue.

Iar. Come forth the Caue: can heauen endure this sight?
Iarbus, curse that vnreuenging *Ioue*,
Whose flintie darts slept in *Tiphous* den,
Whiles these adulterers surfetted with sinne:
Nature, why mad'st me not some poysonous beast,
That with the sharpnes of my edged sting,
I might haue stakte them both vnto the earth,
Whil'st they were sporting in this darksome Caue?

Æn. The ayre is cleere, and Southerne windes are whist,
Come *Dido*, let vs hasten to the towne,
Since gloomie *Æolus* doth cease to frowne.

Dido. Achates and *Ascanius*, well met.

35

Æn. Faire *Anna*, how escapt you from the shower?

Anna. As others did, by running to the wood.

Dido. But where were you *Iarbus* all this while?

Iar. Not with *Æneas* in the vgly Caue.

Dido. I see *Æneas* sticketh in your minde,
But I will soone put by that stumbling blocke,
And quell those hopes that thus employ your cares. *Exeunt.*

Enters Iarbus to Sacrifice.

Iar. Come seruants, come bring forth the Sacrifize,
That I may pacifie that gloomie *Ioue*,
Whose emptie Altars haue enlarg'd our illes.
Eternall *Ioue*, great master of the Clowdes,
Father of gladnesse, and all frollicke thoughts,
That with thy gloomie hand corrects the heauen,
When ayrie creatures warre amongst themselues:
Heare, heare, O heare *Iarbus* plaining prayers,
Whose hideous ecchoes make the welkin howle,
And all the woods *Eliza* to resound:
The woman that thou wild vs entertaine,
Where straying in our borders vp and downe,
She crau'd a hide of ground to build a towne,
With whom we did deuide both lawes and land,
And all the fruites that plentie els sends forth,
Scorning our loues and royall marriage rites,
Yeelds vp her beautie to a strangers bed,
Who hauing wrought her shame, is straight way fled:
Now if thou beest a pitying God of power,
On whom ruth and compassion euer waites,
Redresse these wrongs, and warne him to his ships,
That now afflicts me with his flattering eyes.

Enter Anna.

Anna. How now *Iarbus*, at your prayers so hard?

Iar. I *Anna*, is there ought you would with me?

Anna. Nay, no such waightie busines of import,

But may be slackt vntill another time:
Yet if you would partake with me the cause
Of this deuotion that detaineth you,
I would be thankfull for such curtesie.

Iar. Anna, against this Troian doe I pray,
Who seekes to rob me of thy Sisters loue,
And diue into her heart by coloured lookes.

Anna. Alas poore King that labours so in vaine.
For her that so delighteth in thy paine:
Be rul'd by me, and seeke some other loue,
Whose yeelding heart may yeeld thee more reliefe.

Iar. Mine eye is fixt where fancie cannot start,
O leaue me, leaue me to my silent thoughts,
That register the numbers of my ruth,
And I will either moue the thoughtles flint,
Or drop out both mine eyes in drisling teares,
Before my sorrowes tide haue any stint.

Anna. I will not leaue *Iarbus* whom I loue,
In this delight of dying pensiuenes:
Away with *Dido*, *Anna* be thy song,
Anna that doth admire thee more then heauen.

Iar. I may nor will list to such loathsome chaunge,
That intercepts the course of my desire:
Seruants, come fetch these emptie vessels here,
For I will flye from these alluring eyes,
That doe pursue my peace where ere it goes. *Exit.*

Anna. Iarbus stay, louing *Iarbus* stay,
For I haue honey to present thee with:
Hard hearted, wilt not deigne to heare me speake,
Ile follow thee with outcryes nere the lesse,
And strewe thy walkes with my discheueld haire. *Exit.*

Enter Æneas alone.

Æn. Carthage, my friendly host adue,
Since destinie doth call me from the shoare:
Hermes this night descending in a dreame,
Hath summond me to fruitfull *Italy*:
Ioue wils it so, my mother wils it so:

37

Let my Phenissa graunt, and then I goe:
Graunt she or no, *Æneas* must away,
Whose golden fortunes clogd with courtly ease,
Cannot ascend to Fames immortall house,
Or banquet in bright honors burnisht hall,
Till he hath furrowed *Neptunes* glassie fieldes,
And cut a passage through his toples hilles:
Achates come forth, *Sergestus, Illioneus,*
Cloanthus, haste away, *Æneas* calles.

Enter Achates, Cloanthus, Sergestus, and Illioneus.

Acha. What willes our Lord, or wherefore did he call?

Æn. The dreames (braue mates) that did beset my bed,
When sleepe but newly had imbrast the night,
Commaunds me leaue these vnrenowmed beames,
Whereas Nobilitie abhors to stay,
And none but base *Æneas* will abide:
Abourd, abourd, since Fates doe bid abourd,
And slice the Sea with sable coloured ships,
On whom the nimble windes may all day waight,
And follow them as footemen through the deepe:
Yet *Dido* casts her eyes like anchors out,
To stay my Fleete from loosing forth the Bay:
Come backe, come backe, I heare her crye a farre,
And let me linke my bodie to my lips,
That tyed together by the striuing tongues,
We may as one saile into *Italy.*

Acha. Banish that ticing dame from forth your mouth,
And follow your foreseeing starres in all;
This is no life for men at armes to liue,
Where daliance doth consume a Souldiers strength,
And wanton motions of alluring eyes,
Effeminate our mindes inur'd to warre.

Illio. Why, let vs build a Citie of our owne,
And not stand lingering here for amorous lookes:
Will *Dido* raise old *Priam* forth his graue,
And build the towne againe the Greekes did burne?
No no, she cares not how we sinke or swimme,
So she may haue *Æneas* in her armes.

Cloan. To *Italy*, sweete friends to *Italy,*

We will not stay a minute longer here.

Æn. Troians abourd, and I will follow you,
I faine would goe, yet beautie calles me backe:
To leaue her so and not once say farewell,
Were to transgresse against all lawes of loue:
But if I vse such ceremonious thankes,
As parting friends accustome on the shoare,
Her siluer armes will coll me round about,
And teares of pearle, crye stay, *Æneas*, stay:
Each word she sayes will then containe a Crowne,
And euery speech be ended with a kisse:
I may not dure this female drudgerie,
To sea *Æneas*, finde out *Italy*. *Exit.*

Enter Dido and Anna.

Dido. O *Anna*, runne vnto the water side,
They say *Æneas* men are going abourd,
It may be he will steale away with them:
Stay not to answere me, runne *Anna* runne.
O foolish Troians that would steale from hence,
And not let *Dido* vnderstand their drift:
I would haue giuen *Achates* store of gold,
And *Illioneus* gum and Libian spice,
The common souldiers rich imbrodered coates,
And siluer whistles to controule the windes,
Which *Circes* sent *Sicheus* when he liued:
Vnworthie are they of a Queenes reward:
See where they come, how might I doe to chide?

Enter Anna, with Æneas, Achates, Illioneus, and Sergestus.

Anna. Twas time to runne, *Æneas* had been gone,
The sailes were hoysing vp, and he abourd.

Dido. Is this thy loue to me?

Æn. O princely *Dido*, giue me leaue to speake,
I went to take my farewell *Achates*.

Dido. How haps *Achates* bid me not farewell?

Acha. Because I feard your grace would keepe me here.

Dido. To rid thee of that doubt, abourd againe,
I charge thee put to sea and stay not here.

Acha. Then let *Æneas* goe abourd with vs.

Dido. Get you abourd, *Æneas* meanes to stay.

Æn. The sea is rough, the windes blow to the shoare.

Dido. O false *Æneas*, now the sea is rough,
But when you were abourd twas calme enough,
Thou and *Achates* ment to saile away.

Æn. Hath not the Carthage Queene mine onely sonne?
Thinkes *Dido* I will goe and leaue him here?

Dido. Æneas pardon me, for I forgot
That yong *Ascanius* lay with me this night:
Loue made me iealous, but to make amends,
Weare the emperiall Crowne of *Libia*,
Sway thou the Punike Scepter in my steede,
And punish me *Æneas* for this crime.

Æn. This kisse shall be faire *Didos* punishment.

Dido. O how a Crowne becomes *Æneas* head!
Stay here *Æneas*, and commaund as King.

Æn. How vaine am I to weare this Diadem,
And beare this golden Scepter in my hand?
A Burgonet of steele, and not a Crowne,
A Sword, and not a Scepter fits *Æneas*.

Dido. O keepe them still, and let me gaze my fill:
Now lookes *Æneas* like immortall *Ioue*,
O where is *Ganimed* to hold his cup,
And *Mercury* to flye for what he calles,
Ten thousand *Cupids* houer in the ayre,
And fanne it in *Æneas* louely face,
O that the Clowdes were here wherein thou fleest,
That thou and I vnseene might sport our selues:
Heauens enuious of our ioyes is waxen pale,
And when we whisper, then the starres fall downe,
To be partakers of our honey talke.

Æn. O *Dido*, patronesse of all our liues,
When I leaue thee, death be my punishment,
Swell raging seas, frowne wayward destinies,
Blow windes, threaten ye Rockes and sandie shelfes,
This is the harbour that *Æneas* seekes,
Lets see what tempests can anoy me now.

Dido. Not all the world can take thee from mine armes,
Æneas may commaund as many Moores,
As in the Sea are little water drops:
And now to make experience of my loue,
Faire sister *Anna* leade my louer forth,
And seated on my Gennet, let him ride
As *Didos* husband through the punicke streetes,
And will my guard with Mauritanian darts,
To waite vpon him as their soueraigne Lord.

Anna. What if the Citizens repine thereat?

Dido. Those that dislike what *Dido* giues in charge,
Commaund my guard to slay for their offence:
Shall vulgar pesants storme at what I doe?
The ground is mine that giues them sustenance,
The ayre wherein they breathe, the water, fire,
All that they haue, their lands, their goods, their liues,
And I the Goddesse of all these, commaund
Æneas ride as Carthaginian King.

Acha. *Æneas* for his parentage deserues
As large a kingdome as is *Libia*.

Æn. I, and vnlesse the destinies be false,
I shall be planted in as rich a land.

Dido. Speake of no other land, this land is thine,
Dido is thine, henceforth Ile call thee Lord:
Doe as I bid thee, sister leade the way,
And from a turret Ile behold my loue.

Æn. Then here in me shall flourish *Priams* race,
And thou and I *Achates*, for reuenge,
For *Troy*, for *Priam*, for his fiftie sonnes,
Our kinsmens loues, and thousand guiltles soules,
Will leade an hoste against the hatefull Greekes,
And fire proude *Lacedemon* ore their heads. *Exit.*

41

Dido. Speakes not *Æneas* like a Conqueror?
O blessed tempests that did driue him in,
O happie sand that made him runne aground:
Henceforth you shall be our Carthage Gods:
I, but it may be he will leaue my loue,
And seeke a forraine land calde *Italy*:
O that I had a charme to keepe the windes
Within the closure of a golden ball,
Or that the Tyrrhen sea were in mine armes,
That he might suffer shipwracke on my breast,
As oft as he attempts to hoyst vp saile:
I must preuent him, wishing will not serue:
Goe, bid my Nurse take yong *Ascanius*,
And beare him in the countrey to her house,
Æneas will not goe without his sonne:
Yet left he should, for I am full of feare,
Bring me his oares, his tackling, and his sailes;
What if I sinke his ships? O heele frowne.
Better he frowne, then I should dye for griefe:
I cannot see him frowne, it may not be:
Armies of foes resolu'd to winne this towne,
Or impious traitors vowde to haue my life,
Affright me not, onely *Æneas* frowne
Is that which terrifies poore *Didos* heart:
Nor bloudie speares appearing in the ayre,
Presage the downfall of my Emperie,
Nor blazing Commets threatens *Didos* death,
It is *Æneas* frowne that ends my daies:
If he forsake me not, I neuer dye,
For in his lookes I see eternitie,
And heele make me immortall with a kisse.

Enter a Lord.

Your Nurse is gone with yong *Ascanius*,
And heres *Æneas* tackling, oares and sailes.

Dido. Are these the sailes that in despight of me,
Packt with the windes to beare *Æneas* hence?
Ile hang ye in the chamber where I lye,
Driue if you can my house to *Italy*:
Ile set the casement open that the windes
May enter in, and once againe conspire
Against the life of me poore Carthage Queene:

But though he goe, he stayes in Carthage still,
And let rich Carthage fleete vpon the seas,
So I may haue *Æneas* in mine armes.
Is this the wood that grew in Carthage plaines,
And would be toyling in the watrie billowes,
To rob their mistresse of her Troian guest?
O cursed tree, hadst thou but wit or sense,
To measure how I prize *Æneas* loue,
Thou wouldst haue leapt from out the Sailers hands,
And told me that *Æneas* ment to goe:
And yet I blame thee not, thou art but wood.
The water which our Poets terme a Nimph,
Why did it suffer thee to touch her breast,
And shrunke not backe, knowing my loue was there?
The water is an Element, no Nimph,
Why should I blame *Æneas* for his flight?
O *Dido*, blame not him, but breake his oares,
These were the instruments that launcht him forth,
Theres not so much as this base tackling too,
But dares to heape vp sorrowe to my heart:
Was it not you that hoysed vp these sailes?
Why burst you not, and they fell in the seas?
For this will *Dido* tye ye full of knots,
And sheere ye all asunder with her hands:
Now serue to chastize shipboyes for their faults,
Ye shall no more offend the Carthage Queene,
Now let him hang my fauours on his masts,
And see if those will serue in steed of sailes:
For tackling, let him take the chaines of gold,
Which I bestowd vpon his followers:
In steed of oares, let him vse his hands,
And swim to *Italy*, Ile keepe these sure:
Come beare them in. *Exit.*

Enter the Nurse with Cupid for Ascanius.

Nurse. My Lord *Ascanius*, ye must goe with me.

Cupid. Whither must I goe? Ile stay with my mother.

Nurse. No, thou shalt goe with me vnto my house,
I haue an Orchard that hath store of plums,
Browne Almonds, Seruises, ripe Figs and Dates,
Dewberries, Apples, yellow Orenges,
A garden where are Bee hiues full of honey,

Musk-roses, and a thousand sort of flowers,
And in the midst doth run a siluer streame,
Where thou shalt see the red gild fishes leape,
White Swannes, and many louely water fowles:
Now speake *Ascanius*, will ye goe or no?

Cupid. Come come Ile goe, how farre hence is your house?

Nurse. But hereby child, we shall get thither straight.

Cupid. Nurse I am wearie, will you carrie me?

Nurse. I, so youle dwell with me and call me mother.

Cupid. So youle loue me, I care not if I doe.

Nurse. That I might liue to see this boy a man,
How pretilie he laughs, goe ye wagge,
Youle be a twigger when you come to age.
Say *Dido* what she will I am not old,
Ile be no more a widowe, I am young,
Ile haue a husband, or els a louer.

Cupid. A husband and no teeth!

Nurse. O what meane I to haue such foolish thoughts!
Foolish is loue, a toy, O sacred loue,
If there be any heauen in earth, tis loue:
Especially in women of your yeares.
Blush blush for shame, why shouldst thou thinke of loue?
A graue, and not a louer fits thy age:
A graue, why? I may liue a hundred yeares,
Fourescore is but a girles age, loue is sweete:
My vaines are withered, and my sinewes drie,
Why doe I thinke of loue now I should dye?

Cupid. Come Nurse.

Nurse. Well, if he come a wooing he shall speede,
O how vnwise was I to say him nay! *Exeunt.*

Actus 5.

Enter Æneas with a paper in his hand, drawing the platforme of the citie, with him Achates, Cloanthus, and Illieneus.

Æn. Triumph my mates, our trauels are at end,
Here will *Æneas* build a statelier *Troy*,
Then that which grim *Atrides* ouerthrew:
Carthage shall vaunt her pettie walles no more,
For I will grace them with a fairer frame,
And clad her in a Chrystall liuerie,
Wherein the day may euermore delight:
From golden *India Ganges* will I fetch,
Whose wealthie streames may waite vpon her towers,
And triple wise intrench her round about:
The Sunne from Egypt shall rich odors bring,
Wherewith his burning beames like labouring Bees,
That loade their thighes with *Hyblas* honeys spoyles,
Shall here vnburden their exhaled sweetes,
And plant our pleasant suburbes with her fumes.

Acha. What length or bredth shal this braue towne c=otaine?

Æn. Not past foure thousand paces at the most.

Illio. But what shall it be calde, *Troy* as before?

Æn. That haue I not determinde with my selfe.

Cloan. Let it be term'd *Ænea* by your name.

Serg. Rather *Ascania* by your little sonne.

Æn. Nay, I will haue it calde *Anchisaon*,
Of my old fathers name.

Enter Hermes with Ascanius.

Hermes. Æneas stay, *Ioues* Herald bids thee stay.

Æn. Whom doe I see, *Ioues* winged messenger?
Welcome to *Carthage* new erected towne.

Hermes. Why cosin, stand you building Cities here,
And beautifying the Empire of this Queene,
While *Italy* is cleane out of thy minde?
To too forgetfull of thine owne affayres,
Why wilt thou so betray thy sonnes good hap?
The king of Gods sent me from highest heauen,
To sound this angrie message in thine eares.
Vaine man, what Monarky expectst thou here?
Or with what thought sleepst thou in *Libia* shoare?
If that all glorie hath forsaken thee,
And thou despise the praise of such attempts:
Yet thinke vpon *Ascanius* prophesie,
And yong *Iulus* more then thousand yeares,
Whom I haue brought from *Ida* where he slept,
And bore yong *Cupid* vnto *Cypresse* Ile.

Æn. This was my mother that beguild the Queene,
And made me take my brother for my sonne:
No maruell *Dido* though thou be in loue,
That daylie danlest *Cupid* in thy armes:
Welcome sweet child, where hast thou been this long?

Asca. Eating sweet Comfites with Queene *Didos* maide,
Who euer since hath luld me in her armes.

Æn. Sergestus, beare him hence vnto our ships,
Lest *Dido* spying him keepe him for a pledge.

Hermes. Spendst thou thy time about this little boy,
And giuest not care vnto the charge I bring?
I tell thee thou must straight to *Italy*,
Or els abide the wrath of frowning *Ioue*.

Æn. How should I put into the raging deepe,
Who haue no sailes nor tackling for my ships?
What would the Gods haue me *Deucalion* like,
Flote vp and downe where ere the billowes driue?
Though she repairde my fleete and gaue me ships,
Yet hath she tane away my oares and masts,
And left me neither saile nor sterne abourd.

Enter to them Iarbus.

Iar. How now *Æneas*, sad, what meanes these dumpes?

Æn. Iarbus, I am cleane besides my selfe,
Ioue hath heapt on me such a desperate charge,
Which neither art nor reason may atchieue,
Nor I deuise by what meanes to contriue.

Iar. As how I pray, may I entreat you tell.

Æn. With speede he bids me sail to *Italy*.
When as I want both rigging for my fleete,
And also furniture for these my men.

Iar. If that be all, then cheare thy drooping lookes,
For I will furnish thee with such supplies:
Let some of those thy followers goe with me,
And they shall haue what thing so ere thou needst.

Æn. Thankes good *Iarbus* for thy friendly ayde,
Achates and the rest shall waite on thee,
Whil'st I rest thankfull for this curtesie.

Exit Iarbus and Æneas traine.

Now will I haste vnto *Lauinian* shoare,
And raise a new foundation to old *Troy*,
Witnes the Gods, and witnes heauen and earth,
How loth I am to leaue these *Libian* bounds,
But that eternall *Iupiter* commands.

Enter Dido and Æneas.

Dido. I feare I sawe *Æneas* little sonne,
Led by *Achates* to the Troian fleete:
If it be so, his father meanes to flye:
But here he is, now *Dido* trie thy wit.
Æneas, wherefore goe thy men abourd?,
Why are thy ships new rigd? or to what end
Launcht from the hauen, lye they in the Rhode?
Pardon me though I aske, loue makes me aske.

Æn. O pardon me, if I resolue thee why:
Æneas will not faine with his deare loue,
I must from hence: this day swift *Mercury*
When I was laying a platforme for these walles,
Sent from his father *Ioue*, appeard to me,

47

And in his name rebukt me bitterly,
For lingering here, neglecting *Italy*.

Dido. But yet *Æneas* will not leaue his loue.

Æn. I am commaunded by immortal *Ioue*,
To leaue this towne and passe to *Italy*,
And therefore must of force.

Dido. These words proceed not from *Æneas* heart.

Æn. Not from my heart, for I can hardly goe,
And yet I may not stay, *Dido* farewell.

Dido. Farewell: is this the mends for *Didos* loue?
Doe Troians vse to quit their Louers thus?
Fare well may *Dido*, so *Æneas* stay,
I dye, if my *Æneas* say farewell.

Æn. Then let me goe and neuer say farewell,
Let me goe, farewell, I must from hence.

Dido. These words are poyson to poore *Didos* soule,
O speake like my *Æneas*, like my loue:
Why look'st thou toward the sea? the time hath been
When *Didos* beautie chaungd thine eyes to her;
Am I lesse faire then when thou sawest me first?
O then *Æneas*, tis for griefe of thee:
Say thou wilt stay in *Carthage* with my Queene,
And *Didos* beautie will returne againe:
Æneas, say, how canst thou take thy leaue?
Wilt thou kisse *Dido*? O thy lips haue sworne
To stay with *Dido*: canst thou take her hand?
Thy Hand and mine haue plighted mutuall faith,
Therefore vnkinde *Æneas*, must thou say,
Then let me goe, and neuer say farewell.

Æn. O Queene of *Carthage*, wert thou vgly blacke,
Æneas could not choose but hold thee deare,
Yet must he not gainsay the Gods behest.

Dido. The Gods, what Gods be those that seeke my death?
Wherein haue I offended *Iupiter*,
That he should take *Æneas* from mine armes?
O no, the Gods wey not what Louers doe,

48

It is *Æneas* calles *Æneas* hence,
And wofull *Dido* by these blubbred cheekes,
By this right hand, and by our spousall rites,
Desires *Æneas* to remaine with her:
Si bene quid de te merui, fuit aut tibi quidquam
Dulce meum, miserere domus labentis: & istam
Oro, si quis ad hac precibus locus, exue mentem.

Æn. Desine meque tuis incendere teque querelis,
Italiam non sponte sequor.

Dido. Hast thou forgot how many neighbour kings
Were vp in armes, for making thee my loue?
How *Carthage* did rebell, *Iarbus* storme,
And all the world calles me a second *Helen*,
For being intangled by a strangers lookes:
So thou wouldst proue as true as *Paris* did,
Would, as faire *Troy* was, *Carthage* might be sackt,
And I be calde a second *Helena*.
Had I a sonne by thee, the griefe were lesse,
That I might see *Æneas* in his face:
Now if thou goest, what canst thou leaue behind,
But rather will augment then ease my woe?

Æn. In vaine my loue thou spendst thy fainting breath,
If words might moue me I were ouercome.

Dido. And wilt thou not be mou'd with *Didos* words?
Thy mother was no Goddesse periurd man,
Nor *Dardanus* the author of thy stocke:
But thou art Sprung from *Scythian Caucasus*,
And Tygers of *Hircania* gaue thee sucke:
Ah foolish *Dido* to forbeare this long!
Wast thou not wrackt vpon this *Libian* shoare,
And cam'st to *Dido* like a Fisherswaine?
Repairde not I thy ships, made thee a King,
And all thy needie followers Noblemen?
O Serpent that came creeping from the shoare,
And I for pitie harbord in my bosome,
Wilt thou now slay me with thy venomed sting,
And hisse at *Dido* for preseruing thee?
Goe goe and spare not, seeke out *Italy*,
I hope that that which loue forbids me doe,
The Rockes and Sea-gulfes will performe at large,
And thou shalt perish in the billowes waies,

49

To whom poore *Dido* doth bequeath reuenge,
I traytor, and the waues shall cast thee vp,
Where thou and false *Achates* first set foote:
Which if it chaunce, Ile giue ye buriall,
And weepe vpon your liueles carcases,
Though thou nor he will pitie me a whit.
Why star'st thou in my face? if thou wilt stay,
Leape in mine armes, mine armes are open wide:
If not, turne from me, and Ile turne from thee;
For though thou hast the heart to say farewell,
I haue not power to stay thee: is he gone?
I but heele come againe, he cannot goe,
He loues me to too well to serue me so:
Yet he that in my sight would not relent,
Will, being absent, be abdurate still.
By this is he got to the water side,
And, see the Sailers take him by the hand,
But he shrinkes backe, and now remembring me,
Returnes amaine: welcome, welcome my loue:
But wheres *Æneas*? ah hees gone hees gone!

Anna. What meanes my sister thus to raue and crye?

Dido. O *Anna*, my *Æneas* is abourd,
And leauing me will saile to *Italy*.
Once didst thou goe, and he came backe againe,
Now bring him backe, and thou shalt be a Queene,
And I will liue a priuate life with him.

Anna. Wicked *Æneas*.

Dido. Call him not wicked, sister speake him faire,
And looke vpon him with a Mermaides eye,
Tell him, I neuer vow'd at *Aulis* gulfe
The desolation of his natiue *Troy*,
Nor sent a thousand ships vnto the walles,
Nor euer violated faith to him:
Request him gently (*Anna*) to returne,
I craue but this, he stay a tide or two,
That I may learne to beare it patiently,
If he depart thus suddenly, I dye:
Run *Anna*, run, stay not to answere me.

Anna. I goe faire sister, heauens graunt good successe.

50

Exit Anna.

Enter the Nurse.

Nurse. O *Dido*, your little sonne *Ascanius*
Is gone! he lay with me last night,
And in the morning he was stolne from me,
I thinke some Fairies haue beguiled me.

Dido. O cursed hagge and false dissembling wretch!
That slayest me with thy harsh and hellish tale,
Thou for some pettie guift hast let him goe,
And I am thus deluded of my boy:
Away with her to prison presently,
Traytoresse too keend and cursed Sorceresse.

Nurse. I know not what you meane by treason, I,
I am as true as any one of yours. *Exeunt the Nurse.*

Dido. Away with her, suffer her not to speake.
My sister comes, I like not her sad lookes.

Enter Anna.

Anna. Before I came, *Æneas* was abourd,
And spying me, hoyst vp the sailes amaine:
But I cride out, *Æneas*, false *Æneas* stay.
Then gan he wagge his hand, which yet held vp,
Made me suppose he would haue heard me speake:
Then gan they driue into the Ocean,
Which when I viewd, I cride, *Æneas* stay,
Dido, faire *Dido* wils *Æneas* stay:
Yet he whose heart of adamant or flint,
My teares nor plaints could mollifie a whit:
Then carelesly I rent my haire for griefe,
Which seene to all, though he beheld me not,
They gan to moue him to redresse my ruth,
And stay a while to heare what I could say,
But he clapt vnder hatches saild away.

Dido. O *Anna, Anna*, I will follow him.

Anna. How can ye goe when he hath all your fleete?

Dido. Ile frame me wings of waxe like *Icarus*,

And ore his ships will soare vnto the Sunne,
That they may melt and I fall in his armes:
Or els Ile make a prayer vnto the waues,
That I may swim to him like *Tritons* neece:
O *Anna*, fetch *Orions* Harpe,
That I may tice a Dolphin to the shoare,
And ride vpon his backe vnto my loue:
Looke sister, looke louely *Æneas* ships,
See see, the billowes heaue him vp to heauen,
And now downe falles the keeles into the deepe:
O sister, sister, take away the Rockes,
Theile breake his ships, O *Proteus*, *Neptune*, *Ioue*,
Saue, saue *Æneas*, *Didos* leefest loue!
Now is he come on shoare safe without hurt:
But see, *Achates* wils him put to sea,
And all the Sailers merrie make for ioy,
But he remembring me shrinkes backe againe:
See where he comes, welcome, welcome my loue.

Anna. Ah sister, leaue these idle fantasies,
Sweet sister cease, remember who you are.

Dido. Dido I am, vnlesse I be deceiu'd,
And must I raue thus for a renegate?
Must I make ships for him to saile away?
Nothing can beare me to him but a ship,
And he hath all thy fleete, what shall I doe?
But dye in furie of this ouersight?
I, I must be the murderer of my selfe:
No but I am not, yet I will be straight.
Anna be glad, now haue I found a meane
To rid me from these thoughts of Lunacie:
Not farre from hence there is a woman famoused for arts,
Daughter vnto the Nimphs *Hesperides*,
Who wild me sacrifice his ticing relliques:
Goe *Anna*, bid my seruants bring me fire. *Exit Anna.*

Enter Iarbus.

Iar. How long will *Dido* mourne a strangers flight,
That hath dishonord her and *Carthage* both?
How long shall I with griefe consume my daies,
And reape no guerdon for my truest loue?

Dido. Iarbus, talk not of *Æneas*, let him goe,

Lay to thy hands and helpe me make a fire,
That shall consume all that this stranger left,
For I entend a priuate Sacrifize,
To cure my minde that melts for vnkind loue.

Iar. But afterwards will *Dido* graunt me loue?

Dido. I, I, *Iarbus*, after this is done,
None in the world shall have my loue but thou:
So, leaue me now, let none approach this place. *Exit Iarbus.*
Now *Dido*, with these reliques burne thy selfe,
And make *Æneas* famous through the world,
For periurie and slaughter of a Queene:
Here lye the Sword that in the darksome Caue
He drew, and swore by to be true to me,
Thou shalt burne first, thy crime is worse then his:
Here lye the garment which I cloath'd him in,
When first he came on shoare, perish thou to:
These letters, lines, and periurd papers all,
Shall burne to cinders in this prectious flame.
And now ye Gods that guide the starrie frame,
And order all things at your high dispose;
Graunt, though the traytors land in *Italy*,
They may be still tormented with vnrest,
And from mine ashes let a Conquerour rise,
That may reuenge this treason to a Queene,
By plowing vp his Countries with the Sword:
Betwixt this land and that be neuer league,
Littora littoribus contraria, fluctibus undas
Impresor: arma armis: pugnent ipsig nepotes:
Liue false *Æneas*, truest *Dido* dyes,
Sic sic inuat ire sub umbras.

Enter Anna.

Anna. O helpe *Iarbus*, *Dido* in these flames
Hath burnt her selfe, aye me, vnhappie me!

Enter Iarbus running.

Iar. Cursed *Iarbus*, dye to expiate
The griefe that tires vpon thine inward soule,
Dido I come to thee, aye me *Æneas*.

Anna. What can my teares or cryes preuaile me now?

Dido is dead, *Iarbus* slaine, *Iarbus* my deare loue,
O sweet *Iarbus*, *Annas* sole delight,
What fatall destinie enuies me thus,
To see my sweet *Iarbus* slay himselfe?
But *Anna* now shall honor thee in death,
And mixe her bloud with thine, this shall I doe,
That Gods and men may pitie this my death,
And rue our ends senceles of life or breath;
Now sweet *Iarbus* stay, I come to thee.

FINIS.

Massacre at Paris

by
Christopher Marlowe

DRAMATIS PERSONAE

CHARLES THE NINTH--King of France
Duke of Anjou--his brother, afterwards KING HENRY THE THIRD
King of Navarre
PRINCE OF CONDE--his brother

brothers
DUKE OF GUISE
CARDINAL OF LORRAINE
DUKE DUMAINE

SON TO THE DUKE OF GUISE--a boy
THE LORD HIGH ADMIRAL
DUKE OF JOYEUX
EPERNOUN
PLESHE
BARTUS
TWO LORDS OF POLAND
GONZAGO
RETES
MOUNTSORRELL
COSSINS,--Captain of the King's Guard
MUGEROUN
THE CUTPURSE
LOREINE,--a preacher
SEROUNE
RAMUS
TALEUS
FRIAR
SURGEONENGLISH AGENT
APOTHECARY
Captain of the Guard, Protestants, Schoolmasters, Soldiers,
   Murderers, Attendants, &c.
CATHERINE,--the Queen Mother of France
MARGARET,--her daughter, wife to the KING OF NAVARRE
THE OLD QUEEN OF NAVARRE
DUCHESS OF GUISE
WIFE TO SEROUNE
Maid to the Duchess of Guise

Massacre at Paris

With the Death of the Duke of Guise

Scene I

Enter Charles the French King, Catherine the Queene Mother,
the King of Navarre, the Prince of Condye, the Lord high
Admirall, *and* Margaret the Queene of Navarre, *with others.*

CHARLES. Prince of Navarre my honourable brother,
Prince Condy, and my good Lord Admirall,
wishe this union and religious league,
Knit in these hands, thus joyn'd in nuptiall rites,
May not desolve, till death desolve our lives,
And that the native sparkes of princely love,
That kindled first this motion in our hearts,
May still be feweld in our progenye.

NAVAREE. The many favours which your grace has showne,
From time to time, but specially in this,
Shall binde me ever to your highnes will,
In what Queen Mother or your grace commands.

QUEENE MOTHER. Thanks sonne Navarre, you see we love you
well,
That linke you in mariage with our daughter heer:
And as you know, our difference in Religion
Might be a meanes to crosse you in your love.

CHARLES. Well Madam, let that rest:
And now my Lords the mariage rites perfourm'd,
We think it good to goe and consumate
The rest, with hearing of an holy Masse:
Sister, I think your selfe will beare us company.

QUEENE MARGARET. I will my good Lord.

CHARLES. The rest that will not goe (my Lords) may stay:
Come Mother,
Let us goe to honor this solemnitie.

QUEENE MOTHER. Which Ile desolve with bloud and crueltie.

    [*Aside.*]

    Exit Charles the King, Queene Mother, Margaret
    the Queene of Navar *with others, and manet* Navar,
    the Prince of Condy, *and the* Lord high Admirall.

NAVARRE. Prince Condy and my good Lord Admiral,
Now Guise may storme but does us little hurt:
Having the King, Queene Mother on our side,
To stop the mallice of his envious heart,
That seekes to murder all the Protestants:
Have you not heard of late how he decreed,
If that the King had given consent thereto,
That all the protestants that are in Paris,
Should have been murdered the other night?

ADMIRALL. My Lord I mervaile that th'aspiring Guise
Dares once adventure without the Kings assent,
To meddle or attempt such dangerous things.

CONDY. My Lord you need not mervaile at the Guise,
For what he doth the Pope will ratifie:
In murder, mischeefe, or in tiranny.

NAVARRE. But he that sits and rules above the clowdes,
Doth heare and see the praiers of the just:
And will revenge the bloud of innocents,
That Guise hath slaine by treason of his heart,
And brought by murder to their timeles ends.

ADMIRALL. My Lord, but did you mark the Cardinall
The Guises brother, and the Duke Dumain:
How they did storme at these your nuptiall rites,
Because the house of Burbon now comes in,

And joynes your lineage to the crowne ofFrance?

NAVARRE. And thats the cause that Guise so frowns at us,
And beates his braines to catch us in his trap,
Which he hath pitcht within his deadly toyle.
Come my Lords lets go to the Church and pray,
That God may still defend the right of France:
And make his Gospel flourish in this land.

    Exeunt.

Scene II

    Enter the Duke of Guise.

GUISE. If ever Hymen lowr'd at marriage rites,
And had his alters decks with duskie lightes:
If ever sunne stainde heaven with bloudy clowdes,
And made it look with terrour on the worlde:
If ever day were turnde to ugly night,
And night made semblance of the hue of hell,
This day, this houre, this fatall night,
Shall fully shew the fury of them all.
Apothecarie.--

    Enter the Pothecarie.

POTHECARIE. My Lord.

GUISE. Now shall I prove and guerdon to the ful,
The love thou bear'st unto the house of Guise:
Where are those perfumed gloves which late I sent
To be poysoned, hast thou done them? speake,
Will every savour breed a pangue of death?

POTHECARIE. See where they be my Lord, and he that smelles
but to them, dyes.

GUISE. Then thou remainest resolute.

POTHECARIE. I am my Lord, in what your grace commaundes till death.

GUISE. Thankes my good freend, I wil requite thy love.
Goe then, present them to the Queene Navarre:
For she is that huge blemish in our eye,
That makes these upstart heresies in Fraunce:
Be gone my freend, present them to her straite.
Souldyer.--

    Exit Pothecaier.

    Enter a Souldier.

SOULDIER. My Lord.

GUISE. Now come thou forth and play thy tragick part,
Stand in some window opening neere the street,
And when thou seest the Admirall ride by,
Discharge thy musket and perfourme his death:
And then Ile guerdon thee with store of crownes.

SOULDIER. I will my Lord.

    Exit Souldier.

GUISE. Now Guise, begin those deepe ingendred thoughts
To burst abroad, those never dying flames,
Which cannot be extinguisht but by bloud.
Oft have I leveld, and at last have learnd,
That perill is the cheefest way to happines,
And resolution honors fairest aime.
What glory is there in a common good,
That hanges for every peasant to atchive?
That like I best that flyes beyond my reach.
Set me to scale the high Peramides,
And thereon set the Diadem of Fraunce,
Ile either rend it with my nayles to naught,
Or mount the top with my aspiring winges,

Although my downfall be the deepest hell.
For this, I wake, when others think I sleepe,
For this, I waite, that scorn attendance else:
For this, my quenchles thirst whereon I builde,
Hath often pleaded kindred to the King.
For this, this head, this heart, this hand and sworde,
Contrive, imagine and fully execute
Matters of importe, aimed at by many,
Yet understoode by none.
For this, hath heaven engendred me of earth,
For this, the earth sustaines my bodies weight,
And with this wait Ile counterpoise a Crowne,
Or with seditions weary all the worlde:
For this, from Spaine the stately Catholic
Sends Indian golde to coyne me French ecues:
For this have I a largesse from the Pope,
A pension and a dispensation too:
And by that priviledge to worke upon,
My policye hath framde religion.
Religion: O Diabole.
Fye, I am ashamde, how ever that I seeme,
To think a word of such a simple sound,
Of so great matter should be made the ground.
The gentle King whose pleasure uncontrolde,
Weakneth his body, and will waste his Realme,
If I repaire not what he ruinates:
Him as a childe I dayly winne with words,
So that for proofe, he barely beares the name:
I execute, and he sustaines the blame.
The Mother Queene workes wonders for my sake,
And in my love entombes the hope of Fraunce:
Rifling the bowels of her treasurie,
To supply my wants and necessitie.
Paris hath full five hundred Colledges,
As Monestaries, Priories, Abbyes and halles,
Wherein are thirtie thousand able men,
Besides a thousand sturdy student Catholicks,
And more: of my knowledge in one cloyster keep,
Five hundred fatte Franciscan Fryers and priestes.
All this and more, if more may be comprisde,
To bring the will of our desires to end.
Then Guise,

Since thou hast all the Cardes within thy hands
To shuffle or to cut, take this as surest thing:
That right or wrong, thou deal'st thy selfe a King.
I but, Navarre. Tis but a nook of France.
Sufficient yet for such a pettie King:
That with a rablement of his hereticks,
Blindes Europs eyes and troubleth our estate:
Him will we--

Pointing to his Sworde.

But first lets follow those in France.
That hinder our possession to the crowne:
As Caesar to his souldiers, so say I:
Those that hate me, will I learn to loath.
Give me a look, that when I bend the browes,
Pale death may walke in furrowes of my face:
A hand, that with a graspe may gripe the world,
An eare, to heare what my detractors say,
A royall seate, a scepter and a crowne:
That those which doe behold them may become
As men that stand and gase against the Sunne.
The plot is laide, and things shall come to passe,
Where resolution strives for victory.

Exit.

Scene III

Enter the King of Navar *and* Queen Margaret, *and his olde*
Mother Queen of Navarre, *the* Prince of Condy, *the* Admirall,
and the Pothecary *with the gloves, and gives them to the olde*
Queene.

POTHECARIE. Maddame, I beseech your grace to except this simple
gift.

OLD QUEENE. Thanks my good freend, holde, take thou this reward.

POTHECARIE. I humbly thank your Majestie.

    Exit Pothecary.

OLD QUEENE. Me thinkes the gloves have a very strong perfume,
The sent whereof doth make my head to ake.

NAVARRE. Doth not your grace know the man that gave them you?

OLD QUEENE. Not wel, but do remember such a man.

ADMIRALL. Your grace was ill advisde to take them then,
Considering of these dangerous times.

OLD QUEENE. Help sonne Navarre, I am poysoned.

QUEENE MARGARET. The heavens forbid your highnes such mis-
hap.

NAVARRE. The late suspition of the Duke of Guise,
Might well have moved your highnes to beware
How you did meddle with such dangerous giftes.

QUEENE MARGARET. Too late it is my Lord if that be true
To blame her highnes, but I hope it be
Only some naturall passion makes her sicke.

OLD QUEENE. O no, sweet Margaret, the fatall poyson
Doth work within my heart, my brain pan breakes,
My heart doth faint, I dye.

    She dyes.

NAVARRE. My Mother poysoned heere before my face:
O gracious God, what times are these?
O graunt sweet God my daies may end with hers,
That I with her may dye and live againe.

QUEENE MARGARET. Let not this heavy chaunce my dearest Lord,
(For whose effects my soule is massacred)

Infect thy gracious brest with fresh supply,
To agravate our sodaine miserie.

ADMIRALL. Come my Lords let us beare her body hence,
And see it honoured with just solemnitie.

> *As they are going, enter the Souldier above, who dischargeth*
> *his musket at the Lord Admirall and Exit.*

CONDY. What are you hurt my Lord high Admiral?

ADMIRALL. I my good Lord, shot through the arme.

NAVARRE. We are betraide, come my Lords, and let us goe tell
the King of this.

ADMIRALL. These are the cursed Guisians that doe seeke our death.
Oh fatall was this mariage to us all.

> *They beare away the olde Queene of Navarre and goe out.*

Scene IV

Enter Charles the King, Catherinethe Queene Mother, Duke of
Guise, Duke Anjoy, Duke Demayne *and* Cossin, Captain of the Kings
Guard.

QUEENE MOTHER. My noble sonne, and princely Duke of Guise,
Now have we got the fatall stragling deere,
Within the compasse of a deadly toyle,
And as we late decreed we may perfourme.

CHARLES. Madam, it wilbe noted through the world,
An action bloudy and tirannicall:
Cheefely since under safetie of our word,
They justly challenge their protection:
Besides my heart relentes that noble men,
Onely corrupted in religion,
Ladies of honor, Knightes and Gentlemen,
Should for their conscience taste such rutheles ends.

ANJOY. Though gentle minces should pittie others paines,
Yet will the wisest note their proper greefes:
And rather seeke to scourge their enemies,
Then be themselves base subjects to the whip.

GUISE. Me thinkes my Lord, Anjoy hath well advisde
Your highnes to consider of the thing,
And rather chuse to seek your countries good,
Then pittie or releeve these upstart hereticks.

QUEENE MOTHER. I hope these reasons mayserve my princely,
Sonne,
To have some care for feare of enemies.

CHARLES. Well Madam, I referre it to your Majestie,
And to my Nephew heere the Duke of Guise:
What you determine, I will ratifie.

QUEENE MOTHER. Thankes to my princely sonne, then tell me
Guise,
What order wil you set downe for the Massacre?

GUISE. Thus Madame.
They that shalbe actors in this Massacre,
Shall weare white crosses on their Burgonets,
And tye white linnen scarfes about their armes.
He that wantes these, and is suspect of heresie,
Shall dye, or be he King or Emperour.
Then Ile have a peale of ordinance shot from the tower,
At which they all shall issue out and set the streetes.
And then the watchword being given, a bell shall ring,
Which when they heare, they shall begin to kill:
And never cease untill that bell shall cease,
Then breath a while.

    Enter the Admirals man.

CHARLES. How now fellow, what newes?

MAN. And it please your grace the Lord high Admirall,
Riding the streetes was traiterously shot,
And most humbly intreates your Majestie
To visite him sick in his bed.

CHARLES. Messenger, tell him I will see him straite.

    Exit Messenger.

What shall we doe now with the Admirall?

QUEENE MOTHER. Your Majesty had best goe visite him,
And make a shew as if all were well.

CHARLES. Content, I will goe visite the Admirall.

GUISE. And I will goe take order for his death.

    Exit Guise.

    Enter the Admirall *in his bed.*

CHARLES. How fares it with my Lord high Admiral,
Hath he been hurt with villaines in the street?

I vow and sweare as I am King of France,
To finde and to repay the man with death:
With death delay'd and torments never usde,
That durst presume for hope of any gaine,
To hurt the noble man his sovereign loves.

ADMIRALL. Ah my good Lord, these are the Guisians,
That seeke to massacre our guiltles lives.

CHARLES. Assure your selfe my good Lord Admirall,
I deepely sorrow for your trecherous wrong:
And that I am not more secure my selfe,
Then I am carefull you should be preserved.
Cossin, take twenty of our strongest guarde,
And under your direction see they keep
All trecherous violence from our noble freend,
Repaying all attempts with present death,
Upon the cursed breakers of our peace.
And so be pacient good Lord Admirall,
And every hower I will visite you.*Exeunt* omnes.

Scene V

Enter Guise, Anjoy, Dumaine, Gonzago, Retes, Montsorrell, *and*
Souldiers *to the massacre.*

GUISE. Anjoy, Dumaine, Gonzago, Retes, sweare by
The argent crosses on your burgonets,
To kill all that you suspect of heresie.

DUMAINE. I sweare by this to be unmercifull.

ANJOY. I am disguisde and none nows who I am,
And therfore meane to murder all I meet.

GONZAGO. And so will I.

RETES. And I.

GUISE. Away then, break into the Admirals house.

GETES. I let the Admirall be first dispatcht.

GUISE. The Admirall,
Cheefe standard bearer to the Lutheranes,
Shall in the entrance of this Massacre,
Be murdered in his bed.
Gonzago conduct them hither, and then
Beset his house that not a man may live.

ANJOY. That charge is mine. Swizers keepe you the streetes,
And at ech corner shall the Kings garde stand.

GONZAGO. Come sirs follow me.

   Exit Gonzago *and others with him.*

ANJOY. Cossin, the Captaine of the Admirals guarde,
Plac'd by my brother, will betray his Lord:
Now Guise shall catholiques flourish once againe,
The head being of, the members cannot stand.

RETES. But look my Lord, ther's some in the Admirals house.

   *Enter above Gonzago and others into the Admirals house,
and he in his bed.*

ANJOY. In lucky time, come let us keep this lane,
And slay his servants that shall issue out.

GONZAGO. Where is the Admirall?

ADMIRALL. O let me pray before I dye.

GONZAGO. Then pray unto our Ladye, kisse this crosse.

   Stab him.

ADMIRALL. O God forgive my sins.

GUISE. What, is he dead Gonzago?

GONZAGO. I my Lord.

GUISE. Then throw him down.

[*The body is thrown down. Exeunt* Gonzago *and rest above.*]

ANJOY. Now cosin view him well,
It may be it is some other, and he escapte.

GUISE. Cosin tis he, I know him by his look.
See where my Souldier shot him through the arm.
He mist him neer, but we have strook him now.
Ah base Shatillian and degenerate,
Cheef standard bearer to the Lutheranes,
Thus in despite of thy Religion,
The Duke of Guise stampes on thy liveles bulke.

Away with him, cut of his head and handes,
And send them for a present to the Pope:
And when this just revenge is finished,
Unto mount Faucon will we dragge his coarse:
And he that living hated so the crosse,
Shall being dead, be hangd thereon in chaines.

GUISE. Anjoy, Gonzago, Retes, if that you three,
Will be as resolute as I and Dumaine:
There shall not a Hugonet breath in France.

ANJOY. I sweare by this crosse, wee'l not be partiall,
But slay as many as we can come neer.

GUISE. Mountsorrett, go and shoote the ordinance of,
That they which have already set the street
May know their watchword, and then tole the bell,
And so lets forward to the Massacre.

MOUNTSORRELL. I will my Lord.

Exit Mountsorrell.

GUISE. And now my Lords let us closely to our busines.

ANJOY. Anjoy will follow thee.

DUMAINE. And so will Dumaine.

The ordinance being shot of, the bell tolles.

GUISE. Come then, lets away.

Exeunt.

The Guise enters againe, with all the rest, with their Swords drawne, chasing the Protestants.

GUISE. Tue, tue, tue,
Let none escape, murder the Hugonets.

ANJOY. Kill them, kill them.

Exeunt.

Enter Loreine *running, the* Guise *and the rest pursuing him.*

GUISE. Loreine, Loreine, follow Loreine.. Sirra,
Are you a preacher of these heresies?

LOREINE. I am a preacher of the word of God,
And thou a traitor to thy soule and him.

GUISE. Dearely beloved brother, thus tis written.

He stabs him.

ANJOY. Stay my Lord, let me begin the psalme.

GUISE. Come dragge him away and throw him in a ditch.

Exeunt omnes.

Scene VI

Enter Mountsorrell *and knocks at Serouns doore.*

SEROUNS WIFE. Who is't that knocks there?

[*Within.*]

MOUNTSORRELL. Mountsorrett from the Duke of Guise.

SEROUNS WIFE. Husband come down, heer's one would speak with you from the Duke of Guise.

Enter Seroune.

SEROUNE. To speek with me from such a man as he?

MOUNTSORRELL. I, I, for this Seroune, and thou shalt ha't.

Shewing his dagger.

SEROUNE. O let me pray before I take my death.

MOUNTSORRELL. Despatch then quickly.

SEROUNE. O Christ my Saviour--

MOUNTSORRELL. Christ, villaine?
Why, darst thou presume to call on Christ,
Without the intercession of some Saint?
Sanctus Jacobus hee was my Saint, pray to him.

SEROUNE. O let me pray unto my God.

MOUNTSORRELL. Then take this with you.

Stab him [*and he falls within and dies*].

Exit.

Scene VII

Enter Ramus *in his studie.*

RAMUS. What fearfull cries come from the river Sene,
That fright poore Ramus sitting at his book?
I feare the Guisians have past the bridge,
And meane once more to menace me.

Enter Taleus.

TALEUS. Flye Ramus flye, if thou wilt save thy life.

RAMUS. Tell me Taleus, wherfore should I flye?

TALEUS. The Guisians are hard at thy doore,
And meane to murder us:
Harke, harke they come, Ile leap out at the window.

[Runs out from studie.]

RAMUS. Sweet Taleus stay.

Enter Gonzago and Retes.

GONZAGO. Who goes there?

RETES. Tis Taleus, Ramus bedfellow.

GONZAGO. What art thou?

TALEUS. I am as Ramus is, a Christian.

RETES. O let him goe, he is a catholick.

Exit Taleus.

Enter Ramus *out of his studie.*

GONZAGO. Come Ramus, more golde, or thou shalt have the stabbe.

RAMUS. Alas I am a scholler, how should I have golde?
All that I have is but my stipend from the King,
Which is no sooner receiv'd but it is spent.

Enter the Guise *and* Anjoy [Dumaine, Mountsorrell,
with soldiers].

ANJOY. Whom have you there?

RETES. Tis Ramus, the Kings professor of Logick.

GUISE. Stab him.

RAMUS. O good my Lord,
Wherein hath Ramus been so offencious?

GUISE. Marry sir, in having a smack in all,
And yet didst never sound any thing to the depth.
Was it not thou that scoff'dst the Organon,
And said it was a heape of vanities?
He that will be a flat decotamest,
And seen in nothing but Epitomies:
Is in your judgment thought a learned man.
And he forsooth must goe and preach in Germany:
Excepting against Doctors actions,
And ipse dixi with this quidditie,
Argumentum testimonis est in arte partialis.
To contradict which, I say Ramus shall dye:
How answere you that? your nego argumentum
Cannot serve, Sirrah, kill him.

RAMUS. O good my Lord, let me but speak a word.

ANJOY. Well, say on.

RAMUS. Not for my life doe I desire this pause,
But in my latter houre to purge my selfe,
In that I know the things that I have wrote,
Which as I heare one Shekins takes it ill,
Because my places being but three, contain all his:
I knew the Organon to be confusde,

And I reduc'd it into better forme.
And this for Aristotle will I say,
That he that despiseth him, can nere
Be good in Logick or Philosophie.
And thats because the blockish Sorbonests
Attribute as much unto their workes,
As to the service of the eternall God.

GUISE. Why suffer you that peasant to declaime?
Stab him I say and send him to his freends in hell.

ANJOY. Nere was there Colliars sonne so full of pride.

    Kill him. [*Close the studie.*]

GUISE. My Lord Anjoy, there are a hundred Protestants,
Which we have chaste into the river Sene,
That swim about and so preserve their lives:
How may we doe? I feare me they will live.

DUMAINE. Goe place some men upon the bridge,
With bowes and cartes to shoot at them they see,
And sinke them in the river as they swim.

GUISE. Tis well advisde Dumain, goe see it done.

    Exit Dumaine.

And in the mean time my Lord, could we devise,
To get those pedantes from the King Navarre,
That are tutors to him and the prince of Condy--

ANJOY. For that let me alone, Cousin stay heer,
And when you see me in, then follow hard.

    He knocketh, and enter the King of Navarre and Prince
    of Condy, with their scholmaisters.

How now my Lords, how fare you?

NAVARRE. My Lord, they say
That all the protestants are massacred.

ANJOY. I, so they are, but yet what remedy:
I have done all I could to stay this broile.

NAVARRE. But yet my Lord the report doth run,
That you were one that made this Massacre.

ANJOY. Who I? you are deceived, I rose but now

    Enter [to them] Guise.

GUISE. Murder the Hugonets, take those pedantes hence.

NAVARRE. Thou traitor Guise, lay of thy bloudy hands.

CONDY. Come let us goe tell the King.

    Exeunt [Condy and Navarre].

GUISE. Come sirs, Ile whip you to death with my punniards point.

    He kils them.

ANJOY. Away with them both.

    Exit Anjoy *and soldiers with bodies.*

GUISE. And now sirs for this night let our fury stay.
Yet will we not the Massacre shall end:
Gonzago posse you to Orleance, Retes to Deep,
Mountsorrell unto Roan, and spare not one
That you suspect of heresy. And now stay
That bel that to the devils mattins rings.
Now every man put of his burgonet,
And so convey him closely to his bed.

    Exeunt.

Scene VIII

Enter Anjoy, with two Lords of Poland.

ANJOY. My Lords of Poland I must needs confesse,
The offer of your Prince Elector's, farre
Beyond the reach of my desertes:
For Poland is as I have been enformde,
A martiall people, worthy such a King,
As hath sufficient counsaile in himselfe,
To lighten doubts and frustrate subtile foes.
And such a King whom practice long hath taught,
To please himselfe with mannage of the warres,
The greatest warres within our Christian bounds,
I meane our warres against the Muscovites:
And on the other side against the Turke,
Rich Princes both, and mighty Emperours:
Yet by my brother Charles our King of France,
And by his graces councell it is thought,
That if I undertake to weare the crowne
Of Poland, it may prejudice their hope
Of my inheritance to the crowne of France:
For if th'almighty take my brother hence,
By due discent the Regall seat is mine.
With Poland therfore must I covenant thus,
That if by death of Charles, the diadem
Of France be cast on me, then with your leaves
I may retire me to my native home.
If your commission serve to warrant this,
I thankfully shall undertake the charge
Of you and yours, and carefully maintaine
The wealth and safety of your kingdomes right.

LORD. All this and more your highnes shall commaund,
For Polands crowne and kingly diadem.

ANJOY. Then come my Lords, lets goe.

Exeunt.

Scene IX

Enter two with the Admirals body.

1. Now sirra, what shall we doe with the Admirall?

2. Why let us burne him for a heretick.

1. O no, his bodye will infect the fire, and the fire the aire, and so we shall be poysoned with him.

2. What shall we doe then?

1. Lets throw him into the river.

2. Oh twill corrupt the water, and the water the fish, and the fish our selves when we eate them.

1. Then throw him into the ditch.

2. No, no, to decide all doubts, be rulde by me, lets hang him upon this tree.

1. Agreede.

They hang him.

Enter the Duke of Guise, *and* Queene Mother, *and the* Cardinall of Loraine.

GUISE. Now Madame, how like you our lusty Admirall?

QUEENE MOTHER. Beleeve me Guise he becomes the place so well, That I could long ere this have wisht him there. But come lets walke aside, th'airs not very sweet.

GUISE. No by my faith Madam. Sirs, take him away and throw him in some ditch.

Carry away the dead body.

And now Madam as I understand,
There anre a hundred Hugonets and more,
Which in the woods doe horde their synagogue:
And dayly meet about this time of day,
thither will I to put them to the sword.

QUEENE MOTHER. Doe so sweet Guise, let us delay no time,
For if these straglers gather head againe,
And disperse themselves throughout the Realme of France,
It will be hard for us to worke their deaths.

GUISE. Madam,
I goe as whirl-winces rage before a storme.

   Exit Guise.

QUEENE MOTHER. My Lord of Loraine have you marks of late,
How Charles our sonne begins for to lament
For the late nights worke which my Lord of Guise
Did make in Paris amongst the Hugonites?

CARDINALL. Madam, I have heard him solemnly vow,
With the rebellious King of Navarre,
For to revenge their deaths upon us all.

QUEENE MOTHER. I, but my Lord, let me alone for that,
For Katherine must have her will in France:
As I doe live, so surely shall he dye,
And Henry then shall weare the diadem.
And if he grudge or crosse his Mothers will,
Ile disinherite him and all the rest:
For Ile rule France, but they shall weare the crowne:
And if they storme, I then may pull them downe.
Come my Lord let's goe.

   Exeunt.

Scene X

Enter five or sixe Protestants *with bookes, and kneele together.*

Enter also the Guise *and others.*

GUISE. Downe with the Hugonites, murder them.

PROTESTANT. O Mounser de Guise, heare me but speake.

GUISE. No villain, no that toung of thine,
That hath blasphemde the holy Church of Rome,
Shall drive no plaintes into the Guises eares,
To make the justice of my heart relent:
Tue, tue, tue, let none escape:

Kill them.

So, dragge them away.

Exeunt.

Scene XI

Enter Charles the King of France, Navar and Epernoune
staying him: *Enter* Queene Mother, and the Cardinall of
Loraine, and Pleshe.

CHARLES. O let me stay and rest me heer a while,
A griping paine hath ceasde upon my heart:
A sodaine pang, the messenger of death.

QUEENE MOTHER. O say not so, thou kill'st thy mothers heart.

CHARLES. I must say so, paine forceth me to complain.

NAVARRE. Comfort your selfe my Lord I have no doubt,
But God will sure restore you to your health.

CHARLES. O no, my loving brother of Navarre.
I have deserv'd a scourge I must confesse,
Yet is there pacience of another sort,
Then to misdoe the welfare of their King:
God graunt my neerest freends may prove no worse.
O horde me up, my sight begins to faire,
My sinnewes shrinke, my brain turns upside downe,
My heart doth break, I faint and dye.

He dies.

QUEENE MOTHER. What art thou dead, sweet sonne? speak to thy
Mother.
O no, his soule is fled from out his breast,
And he nor heares, nor sees us what we doe:
My Lords, what resteth now for to be done?
But that we presently despatch Embassadours
To Poland, to call Henry back againe,
To weare his brothers crowne and dignity.
Epernoune, goe see it presently be done,
And bid him come without delay to us.

Epernoune Madam, I will.

Exit Epernoune.

QUEENE MOTHER. And now my Lords after these funerals be done,
We will with all the speed we can, provide
For Henries coronation from Polonia:
Come let us take his body hence.

All goe out, but Navarre and Pleshe.

NAVARRE. And now Navarre whilste that these broiles doe last,
My opportunity may serve me fit,
To steale from France, and hye me to my home.
For heers no saftie in the Realme for me,
And now that Henry is cal'd from Polland,
It is my due by just succession:

And therefore as speedily as I can perfourme,
Ile muster up an army secretdy,
For feare that Guise joyn'd with the King of Spaine,
Might seek to crosse me in mine enterprise.
But God that alwaies doth defend the right,
Will shew his mercy and preserve us still.

PLESHE. The vertues of our poor Religion,
Cannot but march with many graces more:
Whose army shall discomfort all your foes,
And at the length in Pampelonia crowne,
In spite of Spaine and all the popish power,
That hordes it from your highnesse wrongfully:
Your Majestie her rightfull Lord and Soveraigne.

Navarre Truth Pleshe, and God so prosper me in all,
As I entend to labour for the truth,
And true profession of his holy word:
Come Pleshe, lets away while time doth serve.

> *Exeunt.*

Scene XII

> Sound Trumpets within, and then all crye vive le Roy two or
> three times.

> *Enter* Henry crowned: Queene Mother, Cardinall of Loraine,
> Duke of Guise, Epernoone, Mugeroun, the kings Minions, with
> others, and the Cutpurse.

ALL. Vive le Roy, vive le Roy.

> *Sound Trumpets.*

QUEENE MOTHER. Welcome from Poland Henry once agayne,
Welcome to France thy fathers royall seate,

Heere hast thou a country voice of feares,
A warlike people to maintaine thy right,
A watchfull Senate for ordaining lawes,
A loving mother to preserve thy state,
And all things that a King may wish besides:
All this and more hath Henry with his crowne.

CARDINALL. And long may Henry enjoy all this and more.

ALL. Vive le Roy, vive le Roy.

Sound trumpets.

KING. Thanks to you al. The guider of all crownes,
Graunt that our deeds may wel deserve your loves:
And so they shall, if fortune speed my will,
And yeeld our thoughts to height of my desertes.
What say our Minions, think they Henries heart
Will not both harbour love and Majestie?
Put of that feare, they are already joynde,
No person, place, or time, or circumstance,
Shall slacke my loves affection from his bent.
As now you are, so shall you still persist,
Remooveles from the favours of your King.

MUGEROUN. We know that noble minces change not their thoughts
For wearing of a crowne: in that your grace,
Hath worne the Poland diadem, before
You were withvested in the crowne of France.

KING. I tell thee Mugeroun we will be freends,
And fellowes to, what ever stormes arise.

MUGEROUN. Then may it please your Majestie to give me leave,
To punish those that doe prophane this holy feast.

He cuts of the Cutpurse *eare, for cutting of the golde
buttons off his cloake.*

KING. How meanst thou that?

CUTPURSE. O Lord, mine eare.

MUGEROUN. Come sir, give me my buttons and heers your eare.

GUISE. Sirra, take him away.

KING. Hands of good fellow, I will be his baile
For this offence: goe sirra, worke no more,
Till this our Coronation day be past:
And now,
Our rites of Coronation done,
What now remaines, but for a while to feast,
And spend some daies in barriers, tourny, tylte,
And like disportes, such as doe fit the Coutr?
Lets goe my Lords, our dinner staies for us.

Goe out all, but the Queene Mother *and the* Cardinall.

QUEENE MOTHER. My Lord Cardinall of Loraine, tell me,
How likes your grace my sonnes pleasantnes?
His mince you see runnes on his minions,
And all his heaven is to delight himselfe:
And whilste he sleepes securely thus in ease,
Thy brother Guise and we may now provide,
To plant our selves with such authoritie,
That not a man may live without our leaves.
Then shall the Catholick faith of Rome,
Flourish in France, and none deny the same.

Cardinall Madam, as I in secresy was tolde,
My brother Guise hath gathered a power of men,
Which are he saith, to kill the Puritans,
But tis the house of Burbon that he meanest
Now Madam must you insinuate with the King,
And tell him that tis for his Countries good,
And common profit of Religion.

QUEENE MOTHER. Tush man, let me alone with him,
To work the way to bring this thing to passe:
And if he doe deny what I doe say,
Ile dispatch him with his brother presently.
And then shall Mounser weare the diadem.
Tush, all shall dye unles I have my will:

For while she lives Katherine will be Queene.
Come my Lord, let us goe to seek the Guise,
And then determine of this enterprise.

Exeunt.

Scene XIII

Enter the Duchesse of Guise, and her Maide.

DUCHESSE. Goe fetch me pen and inke.

MAID. I will Madam.

Exit Maid.

DUCHESSE. That I may write unto my dearest Lord.
Sweet Mugeroune, tis he that hath my heart,
And Guise usurpes it, cause I am his wife:
Faine would I finde some means to speak with him
But cannot, and therfore am enforst to write,
That he may come and meet me in some place,
Where we may one injoy the others sight.

Enter the Maid *with Inke and Paper.*

So, set it down and leave me to my selfe.
O would to God this quill that heere doth write,

She writes.

Had late been plucks from out faire Cupids wing:
That it might print these lines within his heart.

Enter the Guise.

GUISE. What, all alone my love, and writing too:

I prethee say to whome thou writes?

DUCHESSE. To such a one , as when she reads my lines,
Will laugh I feare me at their good aray.

GUISE. I pray thee let me see.

DUCHESSE. O no my Lord, a woman only must
Partake the secrets of my heart.

GUISE. But Madam I must see.

He takes it.

Are these your secrets that no man must know?

DUCHESSE. O pardon me my Lord.

GUISE. Thou trothles and unjust, what lines are these?
Am I growne olde, or is thy lust growne yong,
Or hath my love been so obscurde in thee,
That others need to comment on my text?
Is all my love forgot which helde thee deare?
I, dearer then the apple of mine eye?
Is Guises glory but a clowdy mist,
In sight and judgement of thy lustfull eye?
Mor du, were not the fruit within thy wombe,
On whose encrease I set some longing hope:
This wrathfull hand should strike thee to the hart
Hence strumpet, hide thy head for shame,
And fly my presence if thou look'st to live.

Exit Duchesse.

O wicked sexe, perjured and unjust,
Now doe I see that from the very first,
Her eyes and lookes sow'd seeds of perjury,
But villaine he to whom these lines should goe,
Shall buy her love even with his dearest bloud.

Exit.

Scene XIV

Enter the King of Navarre, Pleshe *and* Bartus, *and their train,*
with drums and trumpets.

NAVARRE. Now Lords, since in a quarrell just and right,
We undertake to mannage these our warres
Against the proud disturbers of the faith,
I meane the Guise, the Pope, and King of Spaine,
Who set themselves to tread us under foot,
And rend our true religion from this land:
But for you know our quarrell is no more,
But to defend their strange inventions,
Which they will put us to with sword and fire:
We must with resolute minces resolve to fight,
In honor of our God and countries good.
Spaine is the counsell chamber of the pope,
Spaine is the place where he makes peace and warre,
And Guise for Spaine hath now incenst the King,
To send his power to meet us in the field.

BARTUS. Then in this bloudy brunt they may beholde,
The sole endevour of your princely care,
To plant the true succession of the faith,
In spite of Spaine and all his heresies.

NAVARRE. The power of vengeance now implants it selfe,
Upon the hauty mountains of my brest:
Plaies with her goary coulours of revenge,
Whom I respect as leaves of boasting greene,
That change their coulour when the winter comes,
When I shall vaunt as victor in revenge.

Enter a Messenger.

How now sirra, what newes?

MESSENGER. My Lord, as by our scoutes we understande,
A mighty army comes from France with speed:
Which is already mustered in the land,
And meanesto meet your highnes in the field.

NAVARRE. In Gods name, let them come.
This is the Guise that hath incenst the King,
To leavy armes and make these civill broyles:
But canst thou tell me who is their generall?

MESSENGER. Not yet my Lord, for thereon doe they stay:
But as report doth goe, the Duke of Joyeux
Hath made great sute unto the King therfore.

NAVARRE. It will not countervaile his paines I hope,
I would the Guise in his steed might have come,
But he doth lurke within his drousie couch,
And makes his footstoole on securitie:
So he be safe he cares not what becomes,
Of King or Country, no not for them both.
But come my Lords, let us away with speed,
And place our selves in order for the fight.

    Exeunt.

Scene XV

    Enter Henry the King of France, Duke of Guise, Epernoune,
    and Duke Joyeux.

KING. My sweet Joyeux, I make thee Generall,
Of all my army now in readines,
To march against the rebellious King Navarre:
At thy request I am content thou go'st,
Although my love to thee can hardly suffer't,
Regarding still the danger of thy life.

JOYEUX. Thanks to your Majestie, and so I take my leave.
Farwell my Lord of Guise and Epernoune.

GUISE. Health and harty farwell to my Lord Joyeux.

Exit Joyeux.

KING. How kindely Cosin of Guise you and your wife
Doe both salute our lovely Minions.

He makes hornes at the Guise.

Remember you the letter gentle sir,
Which your wife writ to my deare Minion,
And her chosen freend?

GUISE. How now my Lord, faith this is more then need,
Am I to be thus jested at and scornde?
Tis more then kingly or Emperious.
And sure if all the proudest kings beside
In Christendome, should beare me such derision,
They should know I scornde them and their mockes.
I love your Minions? dote on them your selfe,
I know none els but hordes them in disgrace:
And heer by all the Saints in heaven I sweare,
That villain for whom I beare this deep disgrace,
Even for your words that have incenst me so,
Shall buy that strumpets favour with his blood,
Whether he have dishonoured me or no.
Par la mor du, Il mora.

Exit.

KING. Beleeve me, Epernoune this jest bites sore.

EPERNOUNE. My Lord, twere good to make them frends,
For his othes are seldome spent in vaine.

Enter Mugeroun.

KING. How now Mugeroun, metst thou not the Guise at the doore?

MUGEROUN. Not I my Lord, what if I had?

KING. Marry if thou hadst, thou mightst have had the stab,

For he hath solemnely sworne thy death.

MUGEROUN. I may be stabd, and live till he be dead,
But wherfore beares he me such deadly hate?

KING. Because his wife beares thee such kindely love.

MUGEROUN. If that be all, the next time that I meet her,
Ile make her shake off love with her heeles.
But which way is he gone? Ile goe take a walk
On purpose from the Court to meet with him.

 Exit.

KING. I like not this, come Epernoune
Lets goe seek the Duke and make them freends.

 Exeunt.

Scene XVI

 Alarums within. The Duke Joyeux slaine.

 Enter the King of Navarre ,Bartus, and his traine.

NAVARRE. The Duke is slaine and all his power dispearst,
And we are grac'd with wreathes of victory:
Thus God we see doth ever guide the right,
To make his glory great upon the earth.

BARTUS. The terrour of this happy victory,
I hope will make the King surcease his hate:
And either never mannage army more,
Or else employ them in some better cause.

NAVARRE. How many noble men have lost their lives,
In prosecution of these quell armes,
Is ruth and almost death to call to mince:

Put God we know will alwaies put them downe,
That lift themselves against the perfect truth,
Which Ile maintaine as long as life doth last:
And with the Queene of England joyne my force,
To beat the papall Monarck from our lands,
And keep those relicks from our countries coastes.
Come my Lords, now that the storme is overpass,
Let us away with triumph to our tents.

Exeunt.

Scene XVII

Enter a Souldier.

SOULDIER. Sir, to you sir, that dare make the Duke a cuckolde, and use a counterfeite key to his privie Chamber doore: And although you take out nothing but your owne, yet you put in that which displeaseth him, and so forestall his market, and set up your standing where you should not: and whereas tree is your Landlord, you would take upon you to be his, and tyll the ground that he himself should occupy, which is his own free land. If it be not too free there's the question: and though I come not to take possession (as I would I might) yet I meane to keepe you out, which I will if this geare horde: what are ye come so soone? have at ye sir.

Enter Mugeroun.

He shootes at him and killes him.

Enter the Guise *attended.*

GUISE. Holde thee tall Souldier, take thou this and flye.

Exit Souldier.

Lye there the Kings delight, and Guises scorne.
Revenge it Henry as thou list'st or dar'st,
I did it only in despite of thee.

Take him away.

Enter the King *and* Epernoune.

KING. My Lord of Guise, we understand that you
Have gathered a power of men.
What your intent is yet we cannot learn,
But we presume it is not for our good.

GUISE. Why I am no traitor to the crowne of France.
What I have done tis for the Gospel's sake.

EPERNOUNE. Nay for the Popes sake, and shine owne benefite.
What Peere in France but thou (aspiring Guise)
Durst be in armes without the Kings consent?
I challenge thee for treason in the cause.

GUISE. Oh base Epernoune, were not his highnes heere,
Thou shouldst perceive the Duke of Guise is mov'd.

KING. Be patient Guise and threat not Epernoune,
Least thou perceive the King of France be mov'd.

GUISE. Why? I am a Prince of the Valoyses line,
Therfore an enemy to the Burbonites.
I am a juror in the holy league,
And therfore hated of the Protestants.
What should I doe but stand upon my guarde?
And being able, Ile keep an hoast in pay.

EPERNOUNE. Thou able to maintaine an hoast in pay,
That livest by forraine exhibition?
The Pope and King of Spaine are thy good frends,
Else all France knowes how poor a Duke thou art.

KING. I, those are they that feed him with their golde,
To countermaund our will and check our freends.

GUISE. My Lord, to speak more plainely, thus it is:
Being animated by Religious zeale,
I meane to muster all the power I can,
To overthrow those factious Puritans:
And know, the Pope will sell his triple crowne,
I, and the catholick Philip King of Spaine,
Ere I shall want, will cause his Indians,
To rip the golden bowels of America.
Navarre that cloakes them underneath his wings,
Shall feele the house of Lorayne is his foe:
Your highnes need not feare mine armies force,
Tis for your safetie and your enemies wrack.

KING. Guise, weare our crowne, and be thou King of France,
And as Dictator make or warre or peace,

Whilste I cry placet like a Senator.
I cannot brook thy hauty insolence,
Dismisse thy campe or else by our Edict,
Be thou proclaimde a traitor throughout France.

GUISE. The choyse is hard, I must dissemble.

   [*Aside.*]

My Lord, in token of my true humilitie,
And simple meaning to your Majestie,
I kisse your graces hand, and take my leave,
Intending to dislodge my campe with speed.

KING. Then farwell Guise, the King and thou art freends.

   Exit Guise.

EPERNOUNE. But trust him not my Lord,
For had your highnesse seene with what a pompe
He entred Paris, and how the Citizens
With gifts and shewes did entertaine him
And promised to be at his commaund:
Nay, they fear'd not to speak in the streetes,
That Guise ch, durst stand in armes against the King,
For not effecting of his holines will.

KING. Did they of Paris entertaine him so?
Then meanes he present treason to our state.
Well, let me alone, whose within there?

   Enter one with pen and inke.

Make a discharge of all my counsell straite,
And Ile subscribe my name and seale it straight.
My head shall be my counsell, they are false:
And Epernoune I will be rulde by thee.

EPERNOUNE. My Lord,
I think for safety of your person,
It would be good the Guise were made away,
And so to quite your grace of all suspect.

KING. First let us set our hand and seale to this,
And then Ile tell thee what I meane to doe.

He writes.

So, convey this to the counsell presently.

Exit one.

And Epernoune though I seeme milde and calme,
Thinke not but I am tragicall within:
Ile secretly convey me unto Bloyse,
For now that Paris takes the Guises parse,
Heere is not staying for the King of France,
Unles he means to be betraide and dye:
But as I live, so sure the Guise shall dye.

Exeunt.

Scene XVIII

Enter the King of Navarre *reading of a letter, and* Bartus.

NAVARRE. My Lord, I am advertised from France,
That the Guise hath taken armes against the King,
And that Paris is revolted from his grace.

BARTUS. Then hath your grace fit oportunitie,
To shew your love unto the King of France:
Offering him aide against his enemies,
Which cannot but be thankfully receiv'd.

NAVARRE. Bartus, it shall be so, poast then to Fraunce,
And there salute his highnesse in our name,
Assure him all the aide we can provide,
Against the Guisians and their complices.

Bartus be gone, commend me to his grace,
And tell him ere it be long, Ile visite him.

BARTUS. I will my Lord.
  Exit.

NAVARRE. Pleshe.

  Enter Pleshe.
PLESHE. My Lord.

NAVARRE. Pleshe, goe muster up our men with speed,
And let them march away to France amaine:
For we must aide the King against the Guise.
Be gone I say, tis time that we were there.

PLESHE. I goe my Lord.

  [*Exit.*]

NAVARRE. That wicked Guise I feare me much will be,
The wine of that famous Realme of France:
For his aspiring thoughts aime at the crowne,
He takes his vantage on Religion,
To plant the Pope and popelings in the Realme,
And binde it wholy to the Sea of Rome:
But if that God doe prosper mine attempts,
And send us safely to arrive in France:
Wee'l beat him back, and drive him to his death,
That basely seekes the wine of his Realme.

  Exit.

Scene XIX

  Enter the Captaine of the guarde, *and three murtherers.*

CAPTAINE. Come on sirs, what, are you resolutely bent,
Hating the life and honour of the Guise?
What, will you not feare when you see him come?

1. Feare him said you? tush, were he heere, we would kill hin
presently.

2. O that his heart were leaping in my hand.

31. But when will he come that we may murther him?

CAPTAINE. Well then, I see you are resolute.

1. Let us alone, I warrant you.

CAPTAINE. Then sirs take your standings within this Chamber,
For anon the Guise will come.

ALL. You will give us our money?

CAPTAINE. I, I, feare not: stand close, be resolute:

   [*The murtherers go aside as if in the next room.*]

Now fals the star whose influence governes France,
Whose light was deadly to the Protestants:
Now must he fall and perish in his height.

   Enter the King *and* Epernoune.

KING. Now Captain of my guarde, are these murtherers ready?

CAPTAINE. They be my good Lord.

KING. But are they resolute and armde to kill,
Hating the life and honour of the Guise?

CAPTAINE. I warrant you my Lord.

   [*Exit.*]

KING. Then come proud Guise and heere disgordge thy brest,
Surchargde with surfet of ambitious thoughts:
Breath out that life wherein my death was hid,
And end thy endles treasons with thy death.

Enter the Guise [*within*] *and knocketh.*

GUISE. Holla varlet, hey: Epernoune, where is the King?

EPERNOUNE. Mounted his royall Cabonet.

GUISE. I prethee tell him that the Guise is heere.

EPERNOUNE. And please your grace the Duke of Guise doth crave
Accesse unto your highnes.

KING. Let him come in.
Come Guise and see thy traiterous guile outreacht,
And perish in the pit thou mad'st for me.

The Guise *comes to the* King.

GUISE. Good morrow to your Majestie.

KING. Good morrow to my loving Cousin of Guise.
How fares it this morning with your excellence?

GUISE. I heard your Majestie was scarcely pleasde,
That in the Court I bear so great a traine.

KING. They were to blame that said I was displeasde,
And you good Cosin to imagine it.
Twere hard with me if I should doubt my kinne,
Or be suspicious of my deerest freends:
Cousin, assure you I am resolute,
Whatever any whisper in mine eares,
Not to suspect disloyaltye in thee,
And so sweet Cuz farwell.

Exit King *and* Epernoune.

GUISE. So,
Now sues the King for favour to the Guise,
And all his Minions stoup when I commaund:
Why this tis to have an army in the fielde.
Now by the holy sacrament I sweare,
As ancient Romanes over their Captive Lords,

So will I triumph over this wanton King,
And he shall follow my proud Chariots wheeles.
Now doe I but begin to look about,
And all my former time was spent in vaine:
Holde Sworde,
For in thee is the Guises hope.

Enter one of the Murtherers.

Villaine, why cost thou look so gastly? speake.

3. O pardon me my Lord of Guise.

GUISE. Pardon thee, why what hast thou done?

3. O my Lord, I am one of them that is set to murder you.

GUISE. To murder me, villaine?

3. I my Lord, the rest have taine their standings in the next
roome, therefore good my Lord goe not foorth.

GUISE. Yet Caesar shall goe forth.
Let mean consaits, and baser men feare death,
Tut they are pesants, I am Duke of Guise:
And princes with their lookes ingender feare.

2 MURD. Stand close, he is comming, I know him by his voice.

GUISE. As pale as ashes, nay then tis time to look about.

ALL. Downe with him, downe with him.

They stabbe him.

GUISE. Oh I have my death wound, give me leave to speak.

2. Then pray to God, and aske forgivenes of the King.

GUISE. Trouble me not, I neare offended him,
Nor will I aske forgivenes of the King.
Oh that I have not power to stay my life,

Nor immortalitie to be reveng'd:
To dye by Pesantes, what a greefe is this?
Ah Sextus, be reveng'd upon the King,
Philip and Parma, I am slaine for you:
Pope excommunicate, Philip depose,
The wicked branch of curst Valois's line.
Vive la messe, perish Hugonets,
Thus Caesar did goe foorth, and thus he dies.

He dyes.

Enter Captaine of the Guarde.

CAPTAINE. What, have you done?
Then stay a while and Ile goe call the King,

[*Enter* King *and* Epernoune *attended.*]

But see where he comes.
My Lord, see where the Guise is slaine.

KING. Oh this sweet sight is phisick to my soule,
Goe fetch his sonne for to beholde his death:

[*Exit attendant.*]

Surchargde with guilt of thousand massacres,
Mounser of Loraine sinke away to hell,
In just remembrance of those bloudy broyles,
To which thou didst alure me being alive:
And heere in presence of you all I sweare,
I nere was King of France untill this houre:
This is the traitor that hath spent my golde,
In making forraine warres and cruel broiles.
Did he not draw a sorte of English priestes
From Doway to the Seminary at Remes,
To hatch forth treason gainst their naturall Queene?
Did he not cause the King of Spaines huge fleete,
To threaten England and to menace me?
Did he not injure Mounser thats deceast?
Hath he not made me in the Popes defence,
To spend the treasure that should strength my land,

In civill broiles between Navarre and me?
Tush, to be short, he meant to make me Munke,
Or else to murder me, and so be King.
Let Christian princes that shall heare of this,
(As all the world shall know our Guise is dead)
Rest satisfed with this that heer I sweare,
Nere was there King of France so yoakt as I.

EPERNOUNE. My Lord heer is his sonne.

   Enter the Guises sonne.

KING. Boy, look where your father lyes.

YONG GUISE. My father slaine, who hath done this deed?

KING. Sirra twas I that slew him, and will slay
Thee too, and thou prove such a traitor.

YONG GUISE. Art thou King, and hast done this bloudy deed?
Ile be revengde.

   He offereth to throwe his dagger.

KING. Away to prison with him, Ile clippe his winges
Or ere he passe my handes, away with him.

   Exit Boy.

But what availeth that this traitors dead,
When Duke Dumaine his brother is alive,
And that young Cardinall that is growne so proud?
Goe to the Governour of Orleance,
And will him in my name to kill the Duke.

   [*Exit* Captaine of the Guarde.]

Get you away and strangle the Cardinall.

   [*Exit* murtherers.]

These two will make one entire Duke of Guise,

Especially with our olde mothers helpe.

EPERNOUNE. My Lord, see where she comes, as if she droupt
To heare these newest

    Enter Queene Mother *attended.*

KING. And let her croup, my heart is light enough.
Mother, how like you this device of mine?
I slew the Guise, because I would be King.

QUEENE MOTHER. King, why so thou wert before.
Pray God thou be a King now this is done.

KING. Nay he was King and countermanded me,
But now I will be King and rule my selfe,
And make the Guisians stoup that are alive.

QUEENE MOTHER. I cannot speak for greefe: when thou west bome,
I would that I had murdered thee my sonne.
My sonne: thou art a changeling, not my sonne.
I curse thee and exclaime thee miscreant,
Traitor to God, and to the realme of France.

KING. Cry out, exclaime, houle till thy throat be hoarce,
The Guise is slaine, and I rejoyce therefore:
And now will I to armes, come Epernoune:
And let her greeve her heart out if she will.

    Exit the King *and* Epernoune.

QUEENE MOTHER. Away, leave me alone to meditate.
Sweet Guise, would he had died so thou wert heere:
To whom shall I bewray my secrets now,
Or who will helpe to builde Religion?
The Protestants will glory and insulte,
Wicked Navarre will get the crowne of France,
The Popedome cannot stand, all goes to wrack,
And all for thee my Guise: what may I doe?
But sorrow seaze upon my toyling soule,
For since the Guise is dead, I will not live.
                Exit the attendants taking up body of the Guise.

Scene XX

Enter two Murtherers *dragging in the* Cardenall of Loraine.

CARDINALL. Murder me not, I am a Cardenall.

1. Wert thou the Pope thou mightst not scape from us.

CARDINALL. What, will you fyle your handes with Churchmens
bloud?

2. Shed your bloud,
O Lord no: for we entend to strangle you.

CARDINALL. Then there is no remedye but I must dye?

1. No remedye, therefore prepare your selfe.

CARDINALL. Yet lives
My brother Duke Dumaine, and many moe:
To revenge our deaths upon that cursed King,
Upon whose heart may all the furies gripe,
And with their pawes drench his black soule in hell.

1. Yours my Lord Cardinall, you should have saide.

Now they strangle him.

So, pluck amaine,
He is hard hearted, therfore pull with violence.
Come take him away.

Exeunt.

Scene XXI

Enter Duke Dumayn *reading of a letter, with others.*

DUMAINE. My noble brother murthered by the King,
Oh what may I doe, to revenge thy death?
The Kings alone, it cannot satisfie.
Sweet Duke of Guise our prop to leane upon,
Now thou art dead, heere is no stay for us:
I am thy brother, and ile revenge thy death,
And roote Valois's line from forth of France,
And beate proud Burbon to his native home,
That basely seekes to joyne with such a King,
Whose murderous thoughts will be his overthrow.
Hee wild the Governour of Orleance in his name,
That I with speed should have beene put to death.
But thats prevented, for to end his life,
And all those traitors to the Church of Rome,
That durst attempt to murder noble Guise.

Enter the Frier.

FRIER. My Lord, I come to bring you newes, that your brother
the Cardinall of Loraine by the Kings consent is lately strangled
unto death.

DUMAINE. My brother Cardenall slaine and I alive?
O wordes of power to kill a thousand men.
Come let us away and leavy men,
Tis warre that must asswage the tyrantes pride.

FRIER. My Lord, heare me but speak.
I am a Frier of the order of the Jacobyns, that for my
conscience sake will kill the King.

DUMAINE. But what doth move thee above the rest to doe the deed?

FRIER. O my Lord, I have beene a great sinner in my dayes, and
the deed is meritorious.

DUMAINE. But how wilt thou get opportunitye?

FRIER. Tush my Lord, let me alone for that.

DUMAINE. Frier come with me,
We will goe talke more of this within.

Exeunt.

Scene XXII

Sound Drumme and Trumpets, and enter the King of France,
and Navarre, Epernoune, Bartus, Pleshe *and* Souldiers.

KING. Brother of Navarre, I sorrow much,
That ever I was prov'd your enemy,
And that the sweet and princely minde you beare,
Was ever troubled with injurious warres:
I vow as I am lawfull King of France,
To recompence your reconciled love,
With all the honors and affections,
That ever I vouchsafte my dearest freends.

NAVARRE. It is enough if that Navarre may be
Esteemed faithfull to the King of France:
Whose service he may still commaund to death.

KING. Thankes to my Kingly Brother of Navarre.
Then there wee'l lye before Lutetia's walles,
Girting this strumpet Cittie with our siege,
Till surfeiting with our afflicting armes,
She cast her hatefull stomack to the earth.

Enter a Messenger.

MESSENGER. And it please your Majestie heere is a Frier of the
order of the Jacobins, sent from the President of Paris, that
craves accesse unto your grace.

KING. Let him come in.

Enter Frier *with a Letter.*

EPERNOUNE. I like not this Friers look.
Twere not amisse my Lord, if he were searcht.

KING. Sweete Epernoune, our Friers are holy men,
And will not offer violence to their King,
For all the wealth and treasure of the world.
Frier, thou dost acknowledge me thy King?

FRIER. I my good Lord, and will dye therein.

KING. Then come thou neer, and tell what newes thou bringst.

FRIER. My Lord,
The President of Paris greetes your grace,
And sends his dutie by these speedye lines,
Humblye craving your gracious reply.

KING. Ile read them Frier, and then Ile answere thee.

FRIER. Sancte Jacobus, now have mercye on me.

*He stabs the King with a knife as he readeth the letter, and
then the King getteth the knife and killes him.*

EPERNOUNE. O my Lord, let him live a while.

KING. No, let the villaine dye, and feele in hell,
Just torments for his trechery.

NAVARRE. What, is your highnes hurt?

KING. Yes Navarre, but not to death I hope.

NAVARRE. God shield your grace from such a sodaine death:
Goe call a surgeon hether strait.

[Exit attendant.]

KING. What irreligeous Pagans partes be these,
Of such as horde them of the holy church?
Take hence that damned villaine from my sight.

[*Exeunt attendants with body*]

EPERNOUNE. Ah, had your highnes let him live,
We might have punisht him for his deserts.

KING. Sweet Epernoune all Rebels under heaven,
Shall take example by his punishment,
How they beare armes against their soveraigne.
Goe call the English Agent hether strait,
Ile send my sister England newes of this,
And give her warning of her trecherous foes.

[*Enter* Surgeon.]

NAVARRE. Pleaseth your grace to let the Surgeon search your
wound.

KING. The wound I warrant you is deepe my Lord,
Search Surgeon and resolve me what thou seest.

The Surgeon *searcheth.*

Enter the English Agent.

Agent for England, send thy mistres word,
What this detested Jacobin hath done.
Tell her for all this that I hope to live,
Which if I doe, the Papall Monarck goes
To wrack, an antechristian kingdome falles.
These bloudy hands shall teare his triple Crowne,
And fire accursed Rome about his eares.
Ile fire his erased buildings and incense
The papall towers to kisse the holy earth.
Navarre, give me thy hand, I heere do sweare,
To ruinate this wicked Church of Rome,
That hatcheth up such bloudy practices.
And heere protest eternall love to thee,

And to the Queene of England especially,
Whom God hath blest for hating Popery.

NAVARRE. These words revive my thoughts and comfort me,
To see your highnes in this vertuous minde.

KING. Tell me Surgeon, shall I live?

SURGEON. Alas my Lord, the wound is dangerous,
For you are stricken with a poysoned knife.

KING. A poysoned knife? what, shall the French king dye,
Wounded and poysoned, both at once?

EPERNOUNE. O that that damned villaine were alive againe,
That we might torture him with some new found death.

BARTUS. He died a death too good, the devill of hell
Torture his wicked soule.

KING. Oh curse him not since he is dead.
O the fatall poyson workes within my brest,
Tell me Surgeon and flatter not, may I live?

SURGEON. Alas my Lord, your highnes cannot live.

NAVARRE. Surgeon, why saist thou so? the King may live.

KING. Oh no Navarre, thou must be King of France.

NAVARRE. Long may you live, and still be King of France.

EPERNOUNE. Or else dye Epernoune.

KING. Sweet Epernoune thy King must dye. My Lords,
Fight in the quarrell of this valiant Prince,
For he is your lawfull King and my next heire:
Valoyses lyne ends in my tragedie.
Now let the house of Bourbon weare the crowne,
And may it never end in bloud as mine hath done.
Weep not sweet Navarre, but revenge my death.
Ah Epernoune, is this thy love to me?

CHRISTOPHER MARLOWE

Henry thy King wipes of these childish teares,
And bids thee whet thy sword on Sextus bones,
That it may keenly slice the Catholicks.
He loves me not the best that sheds most teares,
But he that makes most lavish of his bloud.
Fire Paris where these trecherous rebels lurke.
I dye Navarre, come beare me to my Sepulchre.
Salute the Queene of England in my name,
And tell her Henry dyes her faithfull freend.

He dyes.

NAVARRE. Come Lords, take up the body of the King,
That we may see it honourably interde:
And then I vow so to revenge his death,
That Rome and all those popish Prelates there,
Shall curse the time that ere Navarre was King,
And rulde in France by Henries fatall death.

They march out with the body of the King, *lying on foure
mens shoulders with a dead march, drawingg weapons on
the ground.*

FINIS.

Also from Benediction Books ...

Wandering Between Two Worlds: Essays on Faith and Art
Anita Mathias
Benediction Books, 2007
152 pages
ISBN: 0955373700

Available from www.amazon.com, www.amazon.co.uk
www.wanderingbetweentwoworlds.com

In these wide-ranging lyrical essays, Anita Mathias writes, in lush, lovely prose, of her naughty Catholic childhood in Jamshedpur, India; her large, eccentric family in Mangalore, a sea-coast town converted by the Portuguese in the sixteenth century; her rebellion and atheism as a teenager in her Himalayan boarding school, run by German missionary nuns, St. Mary's Convent, Nainital; and her abrupt religious conversion after which she entered Mother Teresa's convent in Calcutta as a novice. Later rich, elegant essays explore the dualities of her life as a writer, mother, and Christian in the United States-- Domesticity and Art, Writing and Prayer, and the experience of being "an alien and stranger" as an immigrant in America, sensing the need for roots.

About the Author

Anita Mathias was born in India, has a B.A. and M.A. in English from Somerville College, Oxford University and an M.A. in Creative Writing from the Ohio State University. Her essays have been published in The Washington Post, The London Magazine, The Virginia Quarterly Review, Commonweal, Notre Dame Magazine, America, The Christian Century, Religion Online, The Southwest Review, Contemporary Literary Criticism, New Letters, The Journal, and two of HarperSanFrancisco's The Best Spiritual Writing anthologies. Her non-fiction has won fellowships from The National Endowment for the Arts; The Minnesota State Arts Board; The Jerome Foundation, The Vermont Studio Center; The Virginia Centre for the Creative Arts, and the First Prize for the Best General Interest Article from the Catholic Press Association of the United States and Canada. Anita has taught Creative Writing at the College of William and Mary, and now lives and writes in Oxford, England.

"Yesterday's Treasures for Today's Readers"
Titles by Benediction Classics available from Amazon.co.uk

Religio Medici, Hydriotaphia, Letter to a Friend, Thomas Browne

Pseudodoxia Epidemica: Or, Enquiries into Commonly Presumed Truths, Thomas Browne

Urne Buriall and The Garden of Cyrus, Thomas Browne

The Maid's Tragedy, Beaumont and Fletcher

The Custom of the Country, Beaumont and Fletcher

Philaster Or Love Lies a Bleeding, Beaumont and Fletcher

A Treatise of Fishing with an Angle, Dame Juliana Berners.

Pamphilia to Amphilanthus, Lady Mary Wroth

The Compleat Angler, Izaak Walton

The Magnetic Lady, Ben Jonson

Every Man Out of His Humour, Ben Jonson

The Masque of Blacknesse. The Masque of Beauty,. Ben Jonson

The Life of St. Thomas More, William Roper

Pendennis, William Makepeace Thackeray

Salmacis and Hermaphroditus attributed to Francis Beaumont

Friar Bacon and Friar Bungay Robert Greene

Holy Wisdom, Augustine Baker

The Jew of Malta and the Massacre at Paris, Christopher Marlowe

Tamburlaine the Great, Parts 1 & 2 AND Massacre at Paris, Christopher Marlowe

All Ovids Elegies, Lucans First Booke, Dido Queene of Carthage, Hero and Leander, Christopher Marlowe

The Titan, Theodore Dreiser

Scapegoats of the Empire: The true story of the Bushveldt Carbineers, George Witton

All Hallows' Eve, Charles Williams

The Place of The Lion, Charles Williams

The Greater Trumps, Charles Williams

My Apprenticeship: Volumes I and II, Beatrice Webb

Last and First Men / Star Maker, Olaf Stapledon

Last and First Men, Olaf Stapledon

Darkness and the Light, Olaf Stapledon

The Worst Journey in the World, Apsley Cherry-Garrard

The Schoole of Abuse, Containing a Pleasaunt Invective Against Poets, Pipers, Plaiers, Iesters and Such Like Catepillers of the Commonwelth, Stephen Gosson

Russia in the Shadows, H. G. Wells

Wild Swans at Coole, W. B. Yeats

A hundreth good pointes of husbandrie, Thomas Tusser

The Collected Works of Nathanael West: "The Day of the Locust", "The Dream Life of Balso Snell", "Miss Lonelyhearts", "A Cool Million", Nathanael West

Miss Lonelyhearts & The Day of the Locust, Nathaniel West

The Worst Journey in the World, Apsley Cherry-Garrard

Scott's Last Expedition, V1, R. F. Scott

The Dream of Gerontius, John Henry Newman

The Brother of Daphne, Dornford Yates

The Downfall of Robert Earl of Huntington, Anthony Munday

Clayhanger, Arnold Bennett

The Regent, A Five Towns Story Of Adventure In London , Arnold Bennett

The Card, A Story Of Adventure In The Five Towns , Arnold Bennett

South: The Story of Shackleton's Last Expedition 1914-1917, Sir Ernest Shackketon

Greene's Groatsworth of Wit: Bought With a Million of Repentance, Robert Greene

Beau Sabreur, Percival Christopher Wren

Christ Legends: And Other Stories, Selma Lagerlof; (trans. Velma Swanston Howard)

Chamber Music, James Joyce

Blurt, Master Constable, Thomas Middleton, Thomas Dekker

Since Yesterday, Frederick Lewis Allen

The Scholemaster: Or, Plaine and Perfite Way of Teachyng Children the Latin Tong , Roger Ascham

The Wonderful Year, 1603, Thomas Dekker

Waverley, Sir Walter Scott

Guy Mannering, Sir Walter Scott

Old Mortality, Sir Walter Scott

The Knight of Malta, John Fletcher

The Double Marriage, John Fletcher and Philip Massinger

Space Prison, Tom Godwin

The Home of the Blizzard Being the Story of the Australasian Antarctic Expedition, 1911-1914, Douglas Mawson

Wild-goose Chase , John Fletcher

If You Know Not Me, You Know Nobody. Part I and Part II, Thomas Heywood

The Ragged Trousered Philanthropists, Robert Tressell

The Island of Sheep, John Buchan

Eyes of the Woods, Joseph Altsheler

The Club of Queer Trades, G. K. Chesterton

The Financier, Theodore Dreiser

Something of Myself, Rudyard Kipling

Law of Freedom in a Platform, or True Magistracy Restored, Gerrard Winstanley

Damon and Pithias, Richard Edwards

Dido Queen of Carthage: And, The Massacre at Paris, Christopher Marlowe

Cocoa and Chocolate: Their History from Plantation to Consumer, Arthur Knapp

Lady of Pleasure, James Shirley

The South Pole: An account of the Norwegian Antarctic expedition in the "Fram," 1910-12. Volume 1 and Volume 2, Roald Amundsen

A Yorkshire Tragedy, Thomas Middleton (attrib.)

The Tragedy of Soliman and Perseda, Thomas Kyd

The Rape of Lucrece. Thomas Heywood

Myths and Legends of Ancient Greece and Rome, E. M. Berens

In the Forbidden Land, Henry Savage Arnold Landor

Across Unknown South America, by Arnold Henry Savage Landor

Illustrated History of Furniture: From the Earliest to the Present Time, Frederick Litchfield

A Narrative of Some of the Lord's Dealings with George Müller Written by Himself (Parts I-IV, 1805-1856), George Müller

The Towneley Cycle Of The Mystery Plays (Or The Wakefield Cycle): Thirty-Two Pageants, Anonymous

The Insatiate Countesse, John Marston.

Spontaneous Activity in Education, Maria Montessori.

On the Art of Writing, Sir Arthur Quiller-Couch

The Well of the Saints, J. M. Synge

Bacon's Advancement Of Learning And The New Atlantis, Francis Bacon.

Catholic Tales And Christian Songs, Dorothy Sayers.

Two Little Savages: Being the Adventures of Two Boys who Lived as Indians and What they Learned, Ernest Thompson Seton

The Sadness of Christ, Thomas More

The Family of Love, Thomas Middleton

The Passing of the Aborigines: A Lifetime Spent Among the Natives of Australia, Daisy Bates

The Children, Edith Wharton

A Record of European Armour and Arms through Seven Centuries., Francis Laking

The Book of the Farm: - Detailing The Labours Of The Farmer, Steward, Plowman, Hedger, Cattle-Man, Shepherd, Field-Worker, and Dairymaid. (Volume I). by Henry Stephens

The Book of the Farm: - Detailing The Labours Of The Farmer, Steward, Plowman, Hedger, Cattle-Man, Shepherd, Field-Worker, and Dairymaid. (Volume II). by Henry Stephens

The Book of the Farm: - Detailing The Labours Of The Farmer, Steward, Plowman, Hedger, Cattle-Man, Shepherd, Field-Worker, and Dairymaid. (Volume III). by Henry Stephens

The Naturalist On The River Amazons, by Henry Walter Bates

and many others…

Tell us what you would love to see in print again, at affordable prices!
Email: **benedictionbooks@btinternet.com**

Lightning Source UK Ltd.
Milton Keynes UK
UKOW01f2043190117
292462UK00001B/113/P